DATING for Men and Women (2 BOOK IN 1):

How to Flirt with Men and Women, Boost your Sexual Intelligence,the Art of
Seduction and Sexual Intelligence, FLIRTING: How to Start Conversations like a PRO

Dating for Men (3 Books in 1) :

How to Flirt with Women + Dating Essential for Men + How to Text a Girl : A Complete Guide for Men To Approaching Women With Online Dating

Love Academy

How to Flirt with Women: How to Approach, Flirting, Talk, Attract, Dating and Seduction Women

Love Academy

Disclaimer

All erudition supplied in this book are specified for educational and academic purpose only. The author is not in any way in charge of any outcomes that emerge from utilizing this book. Constructive efforts have been made to render information that is both precise and effective; however, the author is not to be held answerable for the accuracy or use/misuse of this information.

Foreword

I will like to thank you for taking the very first step of trusting me and deciding to purchase/read this life-transforming book. Thanks for investing your time and resources on this product.

I can assure you of precise outcomes if you will diligently follow the specific blueprint I lay bare in the information handbook you are currently checking out. It has transformed lives, and I firmly believe it will equally change your own life too.

All the information I provided in this Do It Yourself piece is easy to absorb and practice.

Table of Contents

INTRODUCTION

At first, we would like to thank you for making this your own. As a man, you are to dream a dream of having a hot beautiful sexy girl as your girlfriend. You might be expensive, smart, intelligent, or handsome, but you can't just ask a lovely lady for a date without convincing her that you deserve her. If you do so, you will find the chance to be a successful deficient. This book can be the guideline for you to make her believe that either she is for you or you deserve her.

It does not mean that I am asking you to believe that it is a book of magic words. I am not claiming that after buying this book, thousands of lovely ladies will leap after you, and you will be dating them one after the other. The truth is that this book will tell you what you need to do and what you must not do to flirt the girl you want.

Another thing is that you should know that to have a date or a courting, you need to flirt with your dream woman. Cunning or look, you would not have purchased this book if you considered your financial capability.

I hope this book is going to give you every theory and practical to tease the beautiful girl you desire. This book is mainly on flirting with a lady. It also highlights how a man must boost himself to make sure that lovely women can observe him. We have also tried our best to allow the readers to know the kind of women that ought to be selected. As you have to choose the lady who suits you, and that can supply you with every little thing you desire from a lovely girl.

So, the book is somewhat qualified to act as the standard for a man to take him closer to his desire girl.

Teasing is necessary to get the girl.

If you can't tease or flirt, she'll see you as "just friends." There will zero sexual stress and zero attractions-- not what you desire.

Flirting is the difference between friendly conversation and sexual conversation. The difference between her seeing you as close friend zone product and her going weak at her knees for you

The power of flirting is suitably summarized in a quote from the television series Mad Men: "You have to let them know the type of man you are, then they'll know what kind of girl to be."

In other words, are you a great, pleasant person or a sex-related man? Are you a close friend zone product or lover material?

Currently, if you're reading this book, you're an awkward flirt. Or possibly you don't have the know-how to flirt at all.

That's okay, because despite appearing like a problematic principle to understanding (I mean, you just flirt., flirting is very simple. As soon as you get the remarkably simple core methods down pat, flirting is not only comfortable but fun.

Before we dive in proper, I wish to give you my sincerest congratulations for taking the very first step in a collection of favorable actions that you will require to absorb order to take control of your dating life. The essential things which you will learn right here regarding ladies and dating are things that I assure you most men in the entire world will not know about their female counterparts. You are offered expertise and information about the greatest keys women have. This consists of details on how ladies think. It includes information on what attracts ladies. It likewise provides info on how you can show the lady around you that you are a great catch, and they must stand and take notice. The book includes details on how to come close to a woman and how to speak to her or chat with her as well as how to keep her connected as you start dating her. There are dating pointers here that many men would disregard.

I make sure that you realize the reason why people will not go out of their way to discover information regarding any subject if they currently think that they have enough info to get the results they desire. After that, what happens when your approaches stop creating the results that you so prefer?

What happens when you recognize that as you age, your methods are not helping you at the same time? Well, at this factor, you have either options. You can choose to continue in your routines and keep doing whatever you are doing even if you know it isn't working well for you and simply expect different results. Or second, you can look for new information that can help you transform your existing behaviors and make much better choices in the future. Yes, the first of these alternatives is reasonably poor, but the second reveals an excellent sign of your character. And picking up this book is just one of those attractive signs!

Bear in mind that many guys proceed with the first (and bad) alternative. The irony of this thought is that it is the same reason why virtually all men fail to discover the most basic and efficient approaches for dating, which you will find in this book.

Happy dating!

CHAPTER ONE

Journey to Flirting

WHY FLIRT?

What's the point of creating sexual tension?

Well, if you don't create sexual tension, you'll probably end up being her friend.

You see, women are like a mirror. If you treat her and speak to her like a friend, you'll become her friend. If you treat her and talk to her like a sexy woman, somebody you wish to have sex with, you'll become her lover.

However, in any case, you will not end up wasting your time as her "friend.") And so, if you wish to bed women, not buddy women, developing sexual tension is a must.

And the best way to develop sexual tension is to flirt. And to flirt? Well, here are two of the best methods, starting with:

What is flirting?

An excellent place to get a response to this question would be the dictionary.

flirt

verb

1. act as though sexually brought into someone, but playfully as opposed to severe objectives

Why Flirt?

To address this inquiry, let's take a look at an instance of a discussion.

where there is no flirtation;

Guy: Where are you from?

Girl: Melbourne!

Guy: Australia? Wow. Did you manage to make it through all the deadly animals?

Girl: Yeah. Laughs.

Guy: Nah, seriously but, I've heard it's one of the world's most livable cities or something. Why would you relocate?

Girl: Yeah, it's a pretty fantastic place to live. I moved because ...".

Blah, blah, blah. And the conversation continues. Notice the problem?

In case you didn't, here's the answer: The conversation is entirely platonic. There is no sexual conversation whatsoever. For all we know, maybe two guys are talking.

To put it bluntly, the guy in the example conversation is going to be going home alone.

And so there you have it, the solution to why flirting is a necessary part of seduction. It gets her picturing the two of you with each other romantically and makes it clear in her mind that you're a sexual guy, not a "just close friends" kind of guy.

Okay, so if flirting is vital to getting ladies to see you as a guy to make love with, and not a "good friend," after that, why are most men nasty at flirting?

Why most Men Suck at Flirting

The men that stay clear of the blunder of not flirting at all (and thus ending up as "just friends"), usually make one of the following mistakes.

For you, this means that as you develop your flirting skills, you'll have another benefit when it comes to seducing the ladies.

Anyhow, here are one of the most typical mistakes people make when flirting

- THEY ARE TOO OBVIOUS.

Many men are simply way also noticeable when it comes to flirting. Why is this a problem?

It sucks the mystery out of the interaction. And along with that, the magic goes excitement. Intrigue is fun, but being obvious kills it.

Below's an example of clumsy, noticeable flirting:

Lady: I enjoy sports bras.

Man: I wager you 'd look outstanding in a sporting activities bra.

Ugh. As well obvious.

So what should flirting resemble instead?

Well, as you'll find in the following chapter, great flirting is much extra refined. It's done with implication rather than specifying things outright. It leaves other enigma and intrigue-- more for women to guess about.

- THEY'RE TOO DIRECT.

Being extremely direct likewise kills the excitement of intrigue.

As an example, this is why it is usually foolish to compliment women based on their physical appearances. (E.g. "You have stunning eyes," or, "Wow, aren't you a stunner?" or, "Are you a model?") Apart from making it appear as though you've never been with an eye-catching lady before (an unattractive trait per se), you kill any mystery you have regarding your purposes.

On top of that, being too direct sexually,(e.g., "I'm going to fuck you so hard later") eliminates a woman's ability to absolve herself of feelings of sluttiness by reasoning that sex "simply happened." Females have been mingled to feel humiliation and fear about being perceived (by either herself, her friends, and even society at large) as "slutty" or sexually promiscuous. So when you're too straight with a woman you've just met and made it clear you're going to bang her, most females bring up some excuse or just disappear. You can consider this as their "anti-slut defense.".

What you need to do instead is give her the means to justify sex as something that "just happened"-- probable deniability. "I've got this amazing pool table at my place; we'll go play around." While you and she both understand what's likely to happen (hint: it begins with "f" and ends with "k"), this example gives her the means to reason it away. She can tell herself that she's merely going to your place to have some fun and see what happens rather than she's going to your site to have sex with you, which would leave her feeling slutty and dirty.

Anyway, so what's the lesson? Do not be so direct!

- **They use friendly chat rather than sex-related flirting.**

You people probably banter a lot if you have a group of male friends. Nevertheless, unless you're gay (which you're probably not if you're reading this book), the small talk isn't going to have any sexual undertones.

Regrettably, for many men, they use this same kind of non-sexual exchange when attempting to flirt.

For example, the difference between sexual and friendly (nonverbal) flirting, think about the difference between giving a girl a "high five" compare to holding hands. One is non-sexual, the other unmistakably sex-related.

Many people take a much less risky path rather than making a robust and high-risk action. This leaves the interactions they have with girls with no sexual undertone.

THE JOURNEY BEGIN.

Flirting with a woman can be a long trip. Sexual never matters excessive if you end up being effective at last. Some guys do not know where the journey should get going. Every man loves to have a chat with the lady he likes. The conversation might just be composed of official greetings like "Hi" and "Hello." Still, the chat can bring a lot of good feelings for him. At the same time, he has to keep in his mind that his journey of flirting with her starts with these official greetings. If your conversations go on and on consisting of just a vocative greeting, she might just put your name in her listing of close friends. She might think this person is just curious about making plain friendships. So you got to attempt to thrill her at your first glimpse. It is precious for you to make a date. You can directly send out the message having your intention if you start flirting with a female after being familiarized with her. You have to tell her directly or indirectly that you are not speaking with her only for making friendship. You need something more. You are asking her for a date. As a result, she will consider you differently than she thinks of other men. You can use all your tricks on her. As she has already had various views on you, now, your techniques of teasing will be confirmed more with the ability to encourage one day. Your journey will take off with a fantastic hope.

Firstly, in your journey, you may not get a cozy welcome from the lady of your dream. You have to be impressive and tranquil. You can not allow her to know how much you are trying to flirt with her. Flirting is a process in which at the end of the day, the lady ends up being desperate for a day. Do not ruin your difficult job by devoting many wrong actions.

19

Understanding Women.

The truth is that guys are virtually not aware of what a woman wants. Without knowing her like or desire, it is impossible to flirt with her. More or less females know very much about a man's wants.

There is no doubt that to flirt with a lady, you have to know what she desires, needs, and wishes. You can not have a date with a lovely woman unless she is impressed.

What women desire in a man

-They want Respect: Women always want respect from men. It is a common idea that is offered in guys that connection is such a thing require to be accomplished, and women can not get that. If the same reasoning is found in you, you can be classified as one of them who believes women as a requirement just for bed-life.

Mindset will indeed never show that you have got respect for them. Ladies can quickly recognize who respects them for real and who does not. Just start to admire them from the heart. Sooner you will discover most of the women are overlooking your other mistakes only for this top quality. They will begin showing interest in you. Even they might want you for their entire life as a partner. So, courting them will be more much easier for you.

-They Want A True Lover: You try the heart and spirit to show yourself as a real enthusiast to the beautiful woman you want to flirt with. Most of the situations, females do not agree to go for a date unless they find their companions love them.

-Make her believe that you can fix all her distresses: In this modern world, women are no more weak sex. Still, they love to believe that their man is qualified to fix any problem they could be passing through. To make her feel this way, you have to concentrate anytime she talks about any of her issues.

-Women like loving and serious guys: Most of the females seek their chances to have a connection with famous writers, actors, singers, and athletes. They like these renowned males because they understand these stars are enthusiastic and sincere. It means that they want their man not only in bed but also in leisure activities and professions.

Having known that you have got lots of interest. She might think that it is time to look at your enthusiasm in the real place, which lies where every woman wants their guy to be passionate most.

-Women want Mr. Dependable: Women are significantly independent nowadays. When it is time to choose a man, they usually neglect it. Every woman wants to depend on her guy and your desired woman, so does it. You try to be a reputable man for her. If you are trustworthy and reliable enough, it always easy to be positive about having a date with you. Because of this, you will have the ability to date her quickly. Firstly, you need to send her the message that you are reliable through your jobs. If your desired lady asks you to do anything for her, it can be sending out emails to someone, getting some books, opening a financial institution account-no issue just how much they look weird to you, try to do the work correctly. She will lose her belief in you if you make a mess of it. She may think she should not have asked you as you are not reliable. Therefore, she could lose some of the tastes she had for you.

-Ladies desire a Man with aPurpose: Women never choose aimless people, as every lady wants her guy eligible to be introduced. They enjoy gossiping. They love to tell others about the job, position, or requirement of their partner. For this, they consider a man having a high passion. So, to flirt with, you can tell her that you are relatively enthusiastic. Do not assume that she is going to think about your words unless she sees you striving to emerge your goal. Do not be late. Allow her to see you pushing hard to acquire an excellent task. Give more than100 percent of you to build a conformist career.

-Lady desires a mindful Guy: Women wish to be cared for. A woman wants his man to be cognizant of her. She desires her male to be caring about her job, research study, needs, and wellness. If her man is reckless about her, she plans to block the road of their relationship. When the game is over, she does not want to be a toy for her man that is thrown away. So you need to be very careful with the woman you intend to flirt with. If she tells you about her illness, you need to go to see her right away. You may stay far away from her, but you need to keep in touch with her in that situation. Speak with her over the phone. Inform her that you are quite worried about her, and you are going to fulfill her immediately. Let her feel that you are incredibly concerned and moved. Also, inform her that you have gone mad to see her. It will create a belief in her that you care for her. It will make her cheer and protected. She will desire this kind of love and treatment for a long time.

Women Need and Desire

Ladies like to desire. They are positive in a playful way. They always want their desire for their life, and they think their men will always get it materialized. It is time for you to discover the hope of the lady you intend to flirt with her.

-Female Enjoys Fairy Stories

We all know that females are warm of opera-soaps, T.V. programs, fairy stories, and charming novels. They want their life to be compared to a fairy story or an enchanting story. You need to allow your desired woman knows that you have come to bring her the best.

-Women Desire for a Hero

Women see a whole lot of Television shows. The lady you desire needs a hero like those programs in her real life. Your girl wants to be enjoyed like a hero enjoys the heroine in flicks or Television shows, and she desires you to be with her in every situation.

-Lady desires to be the best in his man's Eye

Ladies want to be attractive. She wishes her guy not to find another lady more beautiful than she is. If you're going to flirt with a girl, you must not commend the look or shape of another lady in her present.

-Ladies need financial protection

Or else, she might be worried about what her future is going to be if she remains with you. Females always look for economic security. When she understands that you have gotten the ability to satisfy her needs, she might not hesitate to go for a date with you.

-Females want you to be special

Possibly you are not a person that has something in you. Now you have to try to be unique. Ladies always want somebody special. Generally, when a man gets a chance to flirt with a lady, he asks for advice from his nearest and dearest people. The information is practically like "Be yourself "; Think about this guidance. They are of no use. If you do not cohangeyourself, there will be no difference between you and other men. This will not help you. You have to be different; otherwise, the girl you want will not find any type of particular factor for her to approve you as her date and deny others. So, you have to be unique.

A lady might have lots of friends, specifically male friends. Once she figures out that you are attempting something with the same strategies that are familiar to her to excite her, she may be disappointed. To flirt with her, you need to have a specialty in you. You need to be a person that she has never known. Bring changes in her life. To be unique, you need to be one-of-a-kind in every possible means. Expect, the lady you are looking for has invited most of her friends and you at her birthday party. All the invited friends will attend her birthday party with many birthday presents. You have to take it seriously. Invest enough time and get a gift that is going to be unique and gorgeous. Do not go for a ring or pendant. Those are pricey, however productive or not unusual for your purpose. You can go for a little puppy.

 It will be proof of your unique and distinct choice. It might make her think about a different method about you. Hence, you can be a unique one for her.

There are some common subjects and tricks that guys use to impress a girl, and of course, they are well known to ladies by now. As you know, ladies have gotten tastes for flicks and enchanting stories; you may be caught. Females like innovative men.

How To Quickly and Easily Master The Art of flirting
Okay, admittedly, this may look a little bit corny in the beginning, right? I get it. You do not think that you need a personal development tutorial on pseudo-pop-psychology. You believe that the way you see the world is just great. You may be thinking, hurry up and simply tell me how to start flirting and get speaking to women; why in the world has he began talking about the change of mind; why would I need to consider things or check out things differently? Because it's damn important, that's why!

Below are the things; if you watch the world in a certain way, your entire mindset starts to change. Your attitude or the way you assume, whether good or bad, can transform everything in your life.

Favorable psychology scientists are finding that assuming beneficial thoughts and sensations pleasant emotions can help in anxiety management, boost overall health and wellness and well being, and even enhance social and professional skills. Thinking favorably and doing tasks that make you experience positive feelings, not just gives you an instant increase, but the impacts can last much longer after that. Researchers call this the 'widen and build' concept. When you assume favorably or experience excellent feelings, your mind is open to a lot of new opportunities. In an article on the science of hopefulness, James Clear discusses that this, "in turn enables you to construct new abilities and resources that can supply worth in other areas of your life." For you, this suggests that by believing favorably and eliminating negative thoughts and uncertainty, you can get much better at flirting and start attracting more ladies. Potentially even being with something real and significant, if that is what you are after.

Yes, depending on the way you are feeling, you are either sending out an adverse or favorable message to women and everyone. This is why, before we begin anything in this book, you should understand the impact of ideas and how to get assuming positively.

In the simplest terms, if you believe that you can not do it or you are adverse or always anxious, after that, you are setting yourself up for failure. If you are positive and make a selection to delight in life and live it to the fullest, after that, good things will happen. You will give yourself extra chances for success.

Do you wish to find out how to speak with ladies? Do you intend to be confident enough to flirt and even get more dates? Start by developing the appropriate mindset. What have you reached loose? Altering your mindset will drastically change your love life permanently!

The best spot to start is by having a look at how you've been with ladies in previous connections. When you have a good suggestion of what you want, you can see an emphasis on the favorable facets of a person you wish to date and consequently enhance the probabilities of coming close to her and successfully flirting with the right woman.

CHAPTER TWO

Self-development

"Self-Development" offers you more opportunities to flirt with a girl. The fact is you can't change your appearance entirely according to your dream. You may be a guy of a typical occurrence. You can flirt with beautiful women by developing your personality and speaking manner if you wish. These two qualities of a guy have the ability to impress a woman. When you are on a mission to flirt with a girl, these two qualities in you can help you a lot to win your desired girl.

Character advancement.

Your personality is such a thing that can surpass all of your qualities. It creates beauty. You can not establish your nature, just keeping in mind some processes or theories of character development. You need to use whatever you know at the right place and time.

Be Punctual.

Women like punctual people. Do not keep them waiting. If you need some more time to fulfill her than you told her, ask forgiveness from her and just inform her that you are going to be late that day. She might consider you favorably. Do not do it often. If you do so, she may consider it as your wrong usual and you an insincere individual. Punctuality is a fundamental part of your personality.

All set for an outing.

Sitting in a place all the time can make your girl bore. You better take her out. If you are only eager to sit with her in a room, she might consider you a person who does not like to engage with too many things.

Don't ask her many personal questions.

It is a common thing. It destroys your total character. Your desired girl will never like you if you need to know her stuff from her. Nevertheless, you might have the interest, but you better hide them as much as possible. If you can create enough chem, she will open herself as much as you in no time.

Speaking manner.

To flirt with a girl, you must be perfect in your speaking way. Your speaking way can help your desired girl to separate you from other men. Some essential aspects of stabilizing an excellent manner through your speaking are given below:

-Manly Voice.

To flirt with a good looking lady, you got to use your voice completely. Some people have a gifted voice. Their view is deep and positive. This type of view is pleasant to flirt with stunning ladies. Women typically love this kind of male voice. When you discover yourself lacking this manly positive voice, the issue emerges. Still, there is no need to be disappointed. You can make it up. Stand in front of a mirror and start speaking to yourself. Try to get a manly, confident, and deep voice out of your vocal organ. Nowadays, long conversations over phones are very typical between young men and young ladies. Because of this, flirting can be very easy for those who have turned their voice into a developed one.

Less quantity of slung.

When you are flirting with a woman, you can not do it. You can discover other signs of her speech.

You can use double-meaning jokes.

That will be funny to her when you are in front of her and in an early stage of flirting with her; at the same time, you need to be careful about not using slung especially. It might bring a wrong impression on her if you slung exceptionally often in the presence of her. She may think of you negatively. She might avoid you and consider you a bad man and a hot temper. Avoid this habit. Try to be funny. It can be advantageous if you are now a funny man who has a fantastic sense of humor and breaks jokes so often. Women like this sort of man. You can go one action ahead by keeping a smile on her face. You can not create the interest of your desired girl in you unless you make her smile by doing something hilarious.

Don't be too ridiculous.

Sometimes you might act silly to make her laugh. This is never great for you. You need to know that a beautiful woman might choose a ridiculous person only to laugh at all times. Your girl is to date a guy. So, you can not function as a silly person. For this, you need to avoid silly jokes to start with, as ridiculous jokes can typically end up being boring and horrible and make you look immature.

Start talking after she has finished speaking.

You always talk after your girl is completed. Never interrupt her while she is talking. Girls never allow this. They take it as an embarrassment. You might need to wait for long as women love to talk more. If you start talking while she is saying something, she will lose her strength to talk. So, let her talk till she is not done with talking. It will tell her that you have a genuinely excellent way of speaking.

Tease her Often.

Teasing her through your words might be helpful for you to flirt with her. Women like to be teased often by their closest persons but not to be teased in the manner that may disgust her. Remember it; your teasing needs to entertain her. You can tease her, highlighting some kind of sexual meaning out of her words. It can tell her what you are up to.

Confidence.

Self-confidence means your faith in your ability. You must have this quality if you desire to date or court a woman. A guy having confidence is ahead of others in flirting with a woman. When a guy is asked about things he desires in the woman with who he is going to make a date, the possible answer is that she must be beautiful, hot, and attractive. If a woman asks the same question, the reasonable response will be a good-looking and positive man. So, there is no alternative to confidence when you want to flirt with a stunning lady. You need to express through your attitude that you are a guy having an excellent quantity of confidence in yourself whenever you are with the girl you desire.

Increase your self-confidence Level.

To raise your level of confidence, at first, you need to believe yourself better than others in every sphere of life. You will be an exceptional change. Immediately your appearance or your approach towards women will be changed. It will begin to show confidence in you. Some men can not have the courage to flirt with a hot girl. They merely believe that they do not deserve them because they do not have some qualities women want. Get rid of this type of belief as early as possible. Even if you do not have something, you can manage them in time. There is no point in getting disappointed. Be positive and begin to think that you are capable of courting any beautiful girl.

Look Confident.

To look favorable in the eyes of women, you need to bring some changes in your standing, strolling, and making eye contact. As your reputation and strolling typically offer the idea to others about your self-confidence level, you need to do those stated act effectively and very smartly to show self-confidence in you.

As first, you need to make sure that you are getting assistance from nowhere when you are standing. I mean, gradually stand up without leaning. Your weight should be brought by both legs equally. As a result, you will not slump. Slouching is not for them who are positive.

Stroll with the best rate. While strolling serves as a tough guy. Your standing will mean that you do not care about anybody or anything. To get an example of strolling with self-confidence, you can see any popular motion picture where you will find the man standing with confidence.

Over self-confidence.

Overconfidence can work against you. Having a high level of confidence does not mean that you can disregard anybody you like. Always try to stay down. Some men inform their ladies that they are very positive about flirting with the women to show a level of their confidence. Generally, it never works. Women think that they, men simply want to have fun with them. As you know, women always want love; they will never tolerate this type of man. By making this kind of mistake, a guy himself stops his journey to make a date.

The Mindset

To develop a positive mindset, take a minute to consider how you presently feel when you approach a woman. What sort of words entered your mind? For me, it used to be words like a clumsy, bumbling, strange, worried wreck, dirty shoes, wrinkly t-shirt, no aftershave, lousy hair, halitosis, awful, etc. What do you discover? Possibly a bit of an underlying theme of negativeness? I'm ready to bet you if you are honest with yourself, you presently have your variation of negative self-talk and that you believe you could not potentially approach her or that you will get turned down? This kind of unfavorable self-talk is like a self-fulfilling prophecy and, in turn, will likely dictate your result. If you doubted yourself or lacked self-confidence, then you were shooting yourself down before you even started. Your mindset is everything; therefore, it's time to begin feeling excellent about yourself and your flirting approach. Change the unfavorable words with the positive and watch what happens.

Try replacing one unfavorable thought with a positive and view the magic happen.

Attempt stating I can approach that woman. Try looking at the mirror and tell yourself something that you like about your look. Dig deep and develop your most positive characteristics and attributes. This is introspective and might be tough or silly, but I promise you that if you try it, you will open something truly fantastic within you. Doing this will also help you approach and draw in the best woman who is searching for the same favorable qualities you possess. Just try to change one negative belief with a positive one and see how it transform your whole outlook and the reversed sex's outlook towards you!

Society portrays women as the only ones who deal with being positive. Stereotypically, it's presumed that men are simply born positive and, therefore, favorable, but this isn't real. The reality is that men struggle with a favorable mindset and self-love just as much as women. It may not be as spoken about, but it's a problem, on the other hand.

If you're trying to change your dating game or at least be much better with approaching women, then it all starts right here and today. All of it begins with you feeling good about you. Good things will start to happen when you make the shift. Women will start to take notice and will be captivated to see what your positivity is all about. A positive, confident guy is very appealing. You can not only get the kind of relationship you want but likewise produce the life that you always want

Once and for all, just choose to change your mindset!

Take-aways:

- Creating a favorable state of mind is extremely important as it will increase your chances of flirting successfully.

- Positive thinking can help in tension management; improve overall wellness and health, and produce new life skills. Your new skill is flirting!

- Positive mindsets are attractive to women (and men if you want more friends).

You can create a positive frame of mind by:

○   Using the advantages and disadvantages of past relationships to focus on the favorable qualities of a woman you now desire.
○   Replacing negative thoughts and words with positive ones.
○   Focusing on forecasting your highest.
○   Removing unfavorable self-talk to allow you to be effective.

Improving Appearance

If you are too short, you can not be tall in a month.

If your eyes are too small, you can not bring them in an ideal size.

As we know, these things are gifted. You can not change them to improve your appearance. Enhancing your presentation is all about looking your best. Women never miss any sort of small information in men's looks. So, you are to keep your look perfect if you wish to impress your desired girl.

To flirt with a girl, you do not need to be the best-looking person in the world. Just attempt to get the best of you. In this case, a cute hairstyle, smart looking clothing, getting in good shape, and keeping you clean and fresh can be more than useful.

-Clip Your Nails and Get rid of Unwanted Hair

Women like tidy people. They never allow a dirty one for flirting with them. So, keep yourself neat. Clip your nails regularly. Suppose you are with the girl, the girl you wish to flirt with. All of a sudden, you offer her a glass of beverage how will she feel seeing your nails too long and ultimately dirt; it will not be a great scene for her. You, yourself, will also miss some things you need to impress her. You also need to get rid of unwanted hair of your nose and ears, as they often damage the freshness of your look.

To flirt with a girl, try your best to look fresh and fit. In this matter, a shower before going to meet your desired girl will help you a lot. A shower helps everyone to look fresh; Your freshness will attract her.

-Get in A decent shape

I am not saying that you need to have a body like a design or a wrestler to flirt with a girl. You simply require a decent body figure. If you are too fat or thin, women will simply not pay much attention to you. They do not like men who run out of shape. If you currently have a good body, you can be granted as fortunate. Somebody who does not have it needs to work a bit on it. Try to cut down a few of your weight if you are fat.

On the other hand, you require to get a reasonable amount of weight if you are too thin. You can likewise take the help of an excellent trainer to have a good and balanced physique. Accomplish it, and after that, you will discover more women are getting interested in you.

Have a Cool Hair Cut

Women prefer men who have an elegant and up-to-date haircut. Get a hairstyle that fits your look and hair best. A stylish haircut will make you more attractive to the girl you are flirting with. Even an elegant hairstyle will refrain from doing if you do not look after your hair. So, get the right haircut and make your hair look great so that you can draw in the girl you wish to flirt with.

TheSame Clothing in Consecutive Days

Women discover all your look. If you use the same clothes in more than two successive days, your desired girl will notice it ultimately. Women do not like this practice. You might never see a woman who uses the same gown for successive days. They likewise expect the same thing from you. So, do not use the same clothing for consecutive days. Before going to bed, you can choose your next day's dress. Requirement Outfits is vital for you to flirt with the ladies. Great clothes always have a terrific effect on others. Ensure whenever you are in front of your desired girl, your clothing is clean.

Use pleasant smelling mouthwash and fragrance

Always utilize an excellent smelling mouthwash. It will provide you with the self-confidence of getting closer to the girl you want to flirt with. Suppose you have picked a date with her, if you have the confidence of getting your lip closer to her, you will not get the opportunity to kiss her. On the other hand, if she receives a great smell coming from your mouth, she will be interested in coming closer to you. Thus, you will have a perfect date. Use excellent mouthwash and keep yourself set.

A great perfume or a deodorant can offer you the same type of benefits.

Do not forget to use your perfume and antiperspirant before going out.

The things I have told you so far to improve your look are not merely all. Look out for more that can be contributed to make you a better-looking person.

Fear of Rejection

Let me tell you a story about a male. A man fell for a hot and gorgeous girl. He wished to court her at any cost. At the same time, he was scared of getting declined as a result; he stayed quiet. As usual, his silence might not bring him any good news. After a couple of days, he came to know that one of his close friends was attempting to flirt with her. After some days, his friend ended up being effective in courting that beautiful girl. At this news, he was injured terribly, but it was too late for him.

This is a familiar story. Men who have a fear of getting declined, they get the same results the man of the story. You can not escape the outcome of the man in the story unless you get rid of the worry of rejection.

Conquer this fear today

You can easily enjoy the appeal of many beautiful women standing by your window. You can not date any of them by standing there. So, you need to leave your space and be committed to one of the stunning women. As you know by now, after getting engaged, you can start flirting with her. Men who worry about rejection feel that women will let them down. This fear will never let you be with a gorgeous woman. So, overcome it.

A man who is experiencing this fear must understand that he, himself, is developing this fear. He needs to inform himself that getting declined by a beautiful girl is not the end of the world. It happens to everybody; you just need to mature. He needs to take opportunities to flirt with girls. It will be a waste of a chance if he gets turned down. As a man, he is expected to flirt with a girl he desires. Likewise, as a hot woman who you want wishes to be somebody's date. So, the probability of becoming effective is more than being a failure. There is no point in only looking at your desired girl from a distance and getting upset when someone else goes for a date with her. Forgetting every fear, you had better start striking on her today before anybody makes you his competitor.

Just Go With It

All of us know that shit happens. So, being a person, not preferred by luck, you can be turned down from a woman. You must accept it and not be distressed. Maybe the woman who has declined you is simply not "your type." You must carry on with your life and start hoping for the better. Do not stop dreaming of a date with a lovely lady. Once implies missing out one chance, I have already said that getting rejected. Attempt to find out from your previous mistakes and prepare yourself to flirt with another girl once again. Be optimistic while flirting with ladies. Do not be hopeless.

There is always a better one waiting for you. Consider rejection as a chance to get a more stunning girl than that person who declined you. Simply go with it; you are now a mature man.

Be Choosy

Yes, you are a handsome young guy, and you are terribly in need of a woman to make a date. Whatever the situation is, you have to be picky. Unless you end up being selective about discovering your appointment, you can not get a girl of your type. You need to guarantee that the girl you prefer is worthy of all the hard work, money, and time you have invested for her. Because men always run after the appeal of the women, her outlook might interest you most. At the same, you have to learn some other qualities in her that can give you joy. If you do not discover the following attributes in your girl, you better look for another girl who has the following qualities.

-Always sincere to you

Sincerity is an essential quality in a relationship that is required for you to believe her. After becoming your sweetheart, you can ask her many questions to test her whether she is truthful with you or not. Ask her about her person and family life before she becomes your sweetheart. You understand women love to talk. Sooner or later, she may say the fact. So, if she had lied to you, you could have caught her.

-Love you more than your job and money

Women always desire a glamorous life and a better future. For this reason, they prefer rich men. In some cases, lots of gorgeous women pretend to live a rich man or a man having a good job. If you are rich or doing a good job, you need to ensure that your desired girl is not a woman of that type. You can not choose a woman who enjoys your wealth more than you.

Another crucial thing is you must select a woman who listens to your words. Do not just do what she asks you to do. Discover how much validity she holds for you.

-Trusts you a lot

Ensure that the girl you are flirting with trusts you a lot. She is yet to fall in love with you if she does not trust you. Make another thing sure that if she shares every trick of her life to you and something that she has never informed anyone previously. If she shares, she is your girl because women only share their secrets with their confidant and reputable persons.

Be interested in passing more time with you

You should take her out to have some annoyance downtime with her. You need to discover how many times she has asked you for an outing. The more she asks, the more she is interested in you. Choose someone who wishes to have more time with you.

CHAPTER THREE

Learn How to Create that Fun and Flirty Vibes

The primary step in flirting with women is ensuring you begin on the right foot. Your first impression will develop the speed for the rest of your interaction.

You need to comply with some basic rules from the beginning to build the love they keep the mystery and want.

RULE # 1: Don't outrightly show your interest. Most women do not want you to walk up and make a declaration that they are interested in them. That is boring. -- they are already aware.

And how do they become aware?

Because you are in a way showing interest by talking to them, that is enough sign. If you attempt to tell them you are interested directly, it kills the romance.

Men are different from women in aspects of social conduct. Women will talk to any man or girl about anything—even strangers. Guys will just speak with people if there is a reason. If you are talking to a girl as a man, you are surely interested.

RULE # 2: Get going with the flirty vibe. You would like to use humor as a way to begin the flirty vibe. You wish to seem lively, but you also want her to continue doubting whether you love her.

When you generate an atmosphere where she comes back at your comments with some jabs of her own, you can create sexual stress. This is basic psychology. Arousal is stimulation. This is why you might have had a few of the best sex after a significant fight because any friction can create stimulation.

RULE # 3: Confidence is one of the sexiest things you can have. Absolutely nothing is sexier to a woman than you being confident. While it might help your opportunities to have a great deal of money or huge muscles, you can still land an attractive and desirable woman without those things so long as you are confident.

The quantity of confidence you have is built from your interaction and the amount of attraction you can create with a girl.

One of the ways of being confident is making eye contact. Another part is having excellent posture. When you are talking to her, be sure to use her name. Lastly, it is essential to put on a passionate tone. If you end up sounding bored, she will believe you are.

Now you require to make these things a regular part of your character. They expect to stream as easily as a smile. They need to be authentic. That authentic self-confidence comes at putting a high value on who you are as a person.

You can't get phony this. She will see through it rapidly. You have to develop this self-confidence by approaching each new interaction with the state of mind that it does not matter whether she is drawn into you. The less you care, the much better. Tell yourself that you require nothing from her, and it does not matter if she likes you. This is where real self-confidence begins to establish. It looks like a detrimental idea, but it isn't. This will give you the inner confidence needed to play the indirect flirting game women love-- without always further guessing yourself and looking at how well you are doing.

Finally, make sure to take it to a physical level as soon as possible.

Getting From Verbal Flirting to Physical Flirting Fast!

Physical contact is a great way to construct a connection. Physical contact is a great unspoken kind of interaction that clearly states you are interested but keeps the mystery that women love.

Physical contact is good, but it should not be for more than a couple of seconds. A light touch can inform the woman that you are comfortable being close to her. It informs her that you find her attractive. That you are comfy making love, If she touches you in return, it tells her that you are interested in her, and it is okay.

Unlike the other people who have approached her, you are going to leave her wondering:

He hasn't directly said anything, but he appears to be heading out of his way to show he is interested.

He hasn't attempted to impress me, but he keeps touching me, does he like me or not?

This is a significant difference between women and men. Men hate guessing whether or not a woman is interested. If things are uncertain, it pisses men off.

Women are the opposite.

They love the blended signals because it keeps them on their toes. It keeps her thinking.

It gives her a challenge. And most significantly, it is from someone who may not need her attraction.

Building Magnetic Attraction

I make sure you are starting to see that the laws of a destination vary considerably between men and women. Women don't appreciate a man who is too offered. This comes off as a clingy puppy. They also don't desire the all-business direct approach because that eliminates any prospective secret or romance.

You have to be mindful of the indirect approach. It can, in some cases, come off as meek. You want to develop a destination, but you must avoid coming off as meek. You require the slightest "bad young boy" image to build a magnetic tourist attraction.

The fascinating destination is something more powerful than you can imagine. It is the type of target where women can not control.

If you desire to improve your dating life, you require to develop this destination.

Conversation

They say women love to talk. To flirt with a woman, you have to speak to her. Some excellent discussion can impress her easily. Women always try to find men who talk well so that they can have suitable feedback. If you ever get an opportunity to discuss with the girl, you will need to get the best out of that conversation so that she gets interested in you. Below are strategies that will help you to make your discussion fascinating, more protracted, and satisfying to your desired girl.

-Make it longer

Try to talk for a long time whenever you speak to a woman. So, do not offer her the opportunity to finish the discussion with the aid of just two or one "YES" and "NO." You need to ask her questions that will make her talk much to respond. The more she talks with you, the more she gets open up to you. This is what you desire. You ought to give her time when she is making a lengthy conversation, even though her details are not relevant. Do not disappoint her. She may think that you are giving your valuable time just to hear her problems. It may bring luck to you.

Attend to her words

A male always wants to state something that may impress her desired girl. As he takes part in the discussion, he starts to think about what his next sentence is going to be while his girl goes on speaking. It might work against him. As his brain tries to find out what his following sentence is going to be, he can not attend to her words. When the girl finished, he can not connect, or in some cases, he needs to say something irrelevant. This event produces an odd matter for the guy and the lady. So, his desired girl does not get any interest in this type of conversation. He needs to change his conversation technique. He needs to pay a quantity of concentration to the words of his girl so that he can include something pertinent when she finished. As a result, the conversation can move on, ideally.

Be her Assistant

You become the guide for her. Whenever you take your preferred girl to a new place, you manage her. The scenario is different in conversation. When a discussion goes on, the girl rests on the driving seat, not the male. There are two factors behind it. One is, women love to talk, and the other is that women talk much better and organized. Let her speak and just help her so that she can enjoy her talking. After she finished, you can tell her," ultimately said," or "you are satisfied." Such comments will inspire her to talk more to you. She might consider you to be the right person she has been trying to find. If it happens, you are more than a fortunate person.

Usage little Hints

If you wish to have a conversation with a beautiful woman, you can use "little point," she will give you. : you are in a coffee store. All of a sudden, you discover a charming girl in the coffee store. You might have a chat like this:

You: I am much regular in this store. Unfortunately, I have not seen you before.

She: I am new in this town for a research study purpose.

If you use little tip here like "research study purpose," you can make the conversation proceed by asking her about College or University. Therefore your conversation is going to be longer and worthwhile.

Don't bring topic she does not Like

This is a common mistake that nearly every man makes. You ought to not pick subjects for discussion that you like instead, you need to choose items that she likes while discussing with your desired girl. If you bring the subject you want and simply go on talking about it, she will get tired if she does not like the topic. Next time she will reconsider before starting a conversation with you. You better try to understand her favorite topics to discuss. You are a massive fan of football, and your desired girl does not like it that much. She does not have that much understanding of football. If you start talking about what happened last night in the English Premier League, she will merely get no interest in your talking and lose hope in making conversation with you on that subject. It will significantly harm your work. These are the essential things you do not desire.

The less she talks, the less you have opportunities to flirt with her. So, discuss some topics that she likes, and she has a reasonable understanding of that topic. Only then will she show any interest in talking to you. Thus fruitful discussion goes on. You can speak about Television shows, magazines and so on as women primarily favor these subjects. If you do not find any interest in these things, you have to pretend. You need to keep in mind that you are up to something. This is just a little sacrifice for your mission, and it can bring you good luck with a chance of having a date with her.

The power of "Me Too."

Women prefer men who have almost the same kind of disliking and tastes they possess. They delight in the scene whenever a male supports their concepts and ideas.

If you want to be close to her or if you want to flirt with her, you need to develop the routines of uttering the two words, "me too." These two words are strong enough to get a woman's loveliness. These two words from you after saying may need her to think that finally, she has got a man who holds the same kind of likings and disliking as her.

Better not use other lines

While viewing movies or checking out a story, you may find some gorgeous dialogues or lines. You may think you can use any of these to impress the girl who you wish to flirt with. Honestly stating it is exceptionally risky. As you understand women like romance novels and movies, she may determine where you have managed it. Kindly tell her with attractive lines or dialogues, which is the author of those lines or conversations if you do this. And inform her that you also think like this about her. Never try to copy other's paths and make them your own.

Be honest (Women like honesty)- They will never compromise sincerity for anything.

It will create a wrong impression on her. You better depend on your own words. Women love self-dependent and imaginative people.

Make the Move

Just flirting with a beautiful girl can not get satisfaction for any man. He wishes to date her. So, earlier or later, you need to make a move. After being sure about her preferences for you, you can ask her for a trip. When you offer her a date, you ought to look positive. It is much better not to use sentences include words "might," "would," and so on. To draw out my point, I can give you a couple of examples:

You: Can we choose a trip? Please address me.

Or,

You: It is time for us to opt for a trip? What do you think?

You will discover the second one more manly and positive if you compare these two examples. Women want their men to be masculine and confident. So, the second one has more possibility of getting an affirmative reply.

A time will come when the girl who you are flirting with may want you to ask for a date. If you are reluctant or make it late, she will believe that you do not desire it, or you are not brave enough. She will attempt to discover someone else. Do not make it too late.

CHAPTER FOUR

Flirting Do's and Don't

Understanding how to flirt with women can bring substantial changes to your life. Through flirting, many women will believe that you are a fun guy to be with and will want to hang out with you more. If used in the right way, it can even lead to more serious relationships. Men have been flirting with women and vice versa for thousands of years. It is an entirely natural leisure activity.

A lot of flirting includes making the woman feel excellent; the intention must not have to do with sex. By making another person feel pleased, you will also feel more positive about yourself. There are many places that you can flirt; there are social gatherings, workplaces, even when you are traveling.

To start with, you need to know how to use your body movement. By standing close to a woman when talking, and making expressive gestures and casual contact, you will develop a better bond. When talking, it is not wrong to touch a woman on the arm occasionally. As a rule, women are typically more physical than men; therefore do not mind contact unless it is in an overtly sexual nature.

If you are in a congested space, then you can use eye contact to flirt with a woman who might be some distance away. Then interest will develop, and you can approach her if you keep smiling in her instructions and make eye contact over a few hours.

When you fulfill a woman for the first time, avoid cheesy chat lines. Even if she is a stunningly gorgeous woman, you ought to be as natural as possible; complimenting the way she is dressed will make any woman happy!

Flirting with women is a skill that can quickly be developed by any guy. It may take some practice, but ultimately, you will begin to see the results.

Things not to Do

You ought to be technical to approach a woman. There are specific things you need to desist from doing. In this chapter, I will be speaking about the things you need to refrain from doing.

-Do not be too readily available

Try to present yourself as an extremely busy guy in the Eye of your desired girl. Even if you are not busy, you should pretend to be active. By presenting yourself as a busy person, you show that you are leading a life that has more interest. She will know that you are giving her your valuable time only to make her happy. She may be convinced to be with you. Never make yourself that readily available to her.

If she does not make a relationship with you, never tell her that you will be ended up. It will show a weaker personality of you to her. She might not like it. You may be psychological, but do not reveal your complete emotion to her. Women themselves do not like girl type emotional men. You had better avoid this.

After flirting with her for an extended period, you might get used to her interest in you. You should observe her a little bit more if you get the feeling she likes you. If again, you find out that she likes you, but not telling you about her feelings, do not make more hold-up; you need to ask her for a date. Women want to go on a date by men. She might like you, but she waits for you to offer her.

-Never make any commitment

To impress her or to flirt with your desired girl, you can tell her that you are always ready to do anything for her. You better not involve in any commitment with her. She may believe that she has bought you if you get involved in any responsibility with her. Do not be included in dedication.

It is better to not talk for a long time over the phone

You might want to have a discussion when your desired girl over the cell phone when she is not with you. It is prevalent for every guy.

You might have a chat for one or two minutes. You must not talk on the phone for an extended period. It will make her feel that you are someone who has nothing to do but discussing on the phone for hours.

-Never get jealous

You might find your desired girl having time with another person. You may not like the scene as fast as possible you need to conceal your emotion.

Your expression must not reveal that you are jealous.

You must pretend that you are quite liberal about this matter.

You have no business in their relationship. Your jealousy will let her know your possessiveness.

-Women do not like possessive men.

Whenever you are with the girl who you are flirting with, do not pay attention to other gorgeous girls. As you are trying to make, her comprehend that she is the only girl that can make you go crazy. If you are looking at other girls more than her, she will consider you a scam, even a pervert. This is not an excellent thing for your mission.

Once again, women are possessive about their relationship, although they do not like possessive men. So, do not spoil all your hard work making this kind of mistake.

Warning!

-Do not attempt to flirt with women at the funeral service.

- Do not try to flirt with a girl who already has another half or boyfriend.

Most Significant Mistakes Men Make.

Imagine if we were to place a group of random men into a room together and ask each person to say the typical mistakes guys make with ladies, that they are personally guilty of. What would happen?

A man by nature is well delighted to confess their faults when it comes to dating, particularly honestly in the presence of strangers. The first guy may have a difficult time acquiring numbers while the second guy has a problem with keeping women interested. The next person can have a fear of coming close to ladies.

While another man scares ladies away by being an asshole and does not know he's doing it.

Every single one of them would definitely have something that is either difficult or might be boosted.

 Do you even recognize the most significant errors males make with ladies?

How you address those issues does not matter, because no matter what you think now you'll be thinking entirely in a different way by the time you finish reading this list of the top 5 greatest mistakes men make with females and some guidelines to assist curve these harmful routines.

1) Staying in your relationship zone.

That's right, highest on the listing of mistakes men make with women is falling to get beyond their comfort zone and try the new things that are needed to broaden their game along with development. Abandoning your comfort zone is among the hardest achievement when it comes to meeting and dating girls. This is what differentiates the young boys from the men, and the men from the real men. That's due to the reality that it requires extreme games.

Whether it's approaching, intensifying, shutting, or another thing, most of these things are out of the usual for many people, and overcoming this fear of the unknown is the first step to conquer. When you read many success stories and also reach the part where the man begins to improve rapidly, that's typically when he finally breaks out of his comfort zone. That's when a new world opens.

The most useful advice I can give you is to push yourself, but that's all the tips you'll ever require. Press yourself to be incredible, press on your own to make mistakes, media to your straight-out limits. After that, you'll know that what you thought were your restrictions isn't even close to the fact, and you can take it more and if you just keep at it. I'm not going to exist. This process will end up being extremely hard at times, and you'll begin to yearn for the pleasant comfort of mediocrity, but you need to be consistent. The outcomes will come, but just to those that I've gotten it and given it everything they had.

You need to ask yourself:

" Am I going to risk of the regular to accomplish the exceptional?".

Establish your places of interest high and never choose less than you deserve.

Always bear in mind that; If you strive to boost yourself and also your flirt game, after that, you will get results that show the initiative that you are.

That's precisely how the game is played.

2) Being a cock!

Oh yeah, this is a large one. Why would being an asshole be second on our list of mistakes people make with girls? For novices, due to the truth that it usually arises from men attempting to boost their game, not make it tougher to flourish. Many people that are just starting learning more about seduction end up being a considerable penis to a great deal of the ladies they try to flirt.

Why?

This is simple to identify, however not so easy to break the regimen as soon as you have already acquired it. Mostly, when people first locate this web site is among the most attractive ways they find are the ones related to teasing and badgering women. This is because these can get you fast outcomes contrasted to the majority of the different other things, and that doesn't like getting what they want as soon as possible? There's no worry about that, yet it can turn into one when you spend last time improving those methods without making use of anything which is meant to balance it out.

For instance, if you are high at creating and teasing ladies

Don't recognize how to construct comfort and connection; think about what occurs? It makes you look like an asshole. Whether it works against timing or being severe, new men always end up doing it too much. If you push a lady away excessive without knowing how to reel her back in, that's precisely what you're doing at some point:

-Pushing her away forever.

There's no definitive option for this. You merely need to discover your balance by practicing a variety of methods rather than just focusing

on one. That stability varies from man to man, depending on your uniqueness. Some guys can escape more teasing, while others have an easier time creating comfort. The more you practice and establish your flirting game, the more you'll discover more about on your own and also how you need to personalize your game to fit your design and strengths.

Always bear in mind that teasing isn't recommended to be your support approach.

The original goal of it is to construct the first itinerant aim, and you ought to try hard until you achieve your objective,especially when you notice that she is attracted to you it's time to tone it down (not stop entirely, simply unwind a bit)

and also start developing some rapport to work everything out.

You don't want to torture a girl, simply tease her adequate to differentiate yourself from the losers who do not have the spheres to wait on her a bit.

That's as far as it ought to go.

-Teasing excessive is among the biggest mistakes people make with females too often. Make sure to discover appropriate stability in your overall flirting game, so you avoid this significant risk!

3) Concentrating on getting laid

Vagina !!!!!

How helpful is that to you?

Among the awful blunders, men make with women is putting every focus on the wrong objectives and allowing it to handle their concepts and behavior. Generally, that goal is acquiring pussy. If your primary target, just getting laid, making that your crucial emphasis within your mind will genuinely screw with your capacity to run your computer game effectively.

There's no need thinking about it while you're with a female,

as that can limit the chances targeted at getting

the woman right into bed when you need to be using your full ability. When you go out wishing to meet females, some instances of great objectives to have are:

-Enjoying, satisfying people, enhancing your computer game as well as boosting your social worth.

Some cases of contrary goals when you go out to meet women to have are:

Getting laid this night, the number of times you get, flaunting, and resembling you're the guy.

Because this does not mean those are the wrong objectives to have, fairly the contrary. They're wrong to focus too much. Merely by going out to having fun and meet new ladies, you'll be getting great deals of numbers, looking like the man to getting laid. It's about your state of mind.

4) Putting cuffs on a woman.

Guys that are just finding the game tend to get recorded captivated with the first woman that they successfully use their new skills on. This is among the typical errors guys make with women that can be exceptionally hard to be clear of if you're new to these things. They after that, they concentrate on that specific one girl that they overlook to keep exercising and also advancing their game. They assume they're done.

There's nothing wrong with falling in love, and it is possible that the very first woman you achieve success at shutting can be "the one."

You'll forget every little thing if you allow one woman to manage your sincerity you know about the real game and start making a shitload of blunders, such as:

You'll try to keep tabs on what she's doing.

Acquire jealous worrying different other guys being around her.

Fret about her leaving you or wearying.

Do everything she wants to like her little bitch.

The paradox behind this is that you'll be making all of these blunders to stay away from something unfavorable occurrence. Yet, your characters will be what makes things you are afraid od end up taking place for real.

When you get a lady, the game does not end. It's just started.

5) Promising, not giving.

I've observed that a lot of people will state things like:

" Yeah, I'm conceited."

" Money isn't an issue for me."

Or "I'm mean too sure for that."

Rather than showing their beneficial qualities through their doings, some ignorant men will try to express them to thrill women. This is one of the greatest blunders men make with women, however one that can be quickly avoided. That's why it's just number 5 if you aren't boasting.

Deliberately, you need not to describe your enticing vocally.

Do not reveal your qualities to a woman. It's a bad idea. Instead, show her through your actions.

Throughout the PUA area, we tend to spray words like "player" and "confident" as well as "alpha," but you ought not to directly notify a girl you're any one of those things. It will not impress or attract her.

If that had not, doing so will make it look like you're bragging even been your function. Believe me; if you are a cocky, specific guy who has a lot of money, you have no reason to say it.

Just by communicating with a woman for a while, she will detect and discover each of those things on her own, which is the natural action it should take and will make a better perception to her. What you assume is much more impressive to a woman, telling her you have a Range Rover when you first met or appearing in your Range Rover along with shocking her when you check out to pick her up for the first day? The only reliable way to verbally provide your excellent traits is by telling stories instead of being so specific.

Doing it in this manner will typically stop it from getting the bragging label because the essential things that you say are simply "a part of the story." However, that isn't the best means to do it; if you want a girl to know something surprising about you, revealing it to her will be better than trying to notify her about it.

Well, there you have it, the leading five mistakes men prevent them.

The Rule of Flirting

Don'ts:

Do not appeal to get the desire or regard of a woman. This means no buying her drinks at a bar or offer to drive totally out of your ways for her. There is no reasoning dealing with a girl that you have fact just known for a couple of weeks like a princess. You ought to go ahead and make an actual observation to guarantee she is putting forth a minimum of 50% of the effort in keeping the long-term relationship.

-Don'tplace her on a pedestal.

Recognize that you as well have worth and needs to work towards.

-Don't be scared to disagree or tease her playfully. It's necessary to activate the position in her. It shows that you have self-confidence; it helps prevent you from putting her on a stand. She's a human being with concerns & problems much like everyone else.

-Don't tell a girl too much about only how you feel ahead of time in the relationship. - Mainstream media will always ask you to share your feelings and say to the woman how you feel. This is a substantial mistake, as she will certainly see you as a weak doormat.

Do not speak to her on the phone, message, or Facebook for hours at a time.

Always have something much better to do than hang around talking with a woman, such as using a false time restraint to leave conversation where possible. The principle is to leave them on a high note, advocating more. SMS message and call need only to be scheduled for specified days and meetings as well as talking with her in reality.

-Do not over-analyze everything. An example consists of "OMG, she touched my leg. She wants me," Girls can tell when you're into them, and you need to have the ability to say if they enjoy you. Suppose you can't know if she enjoys you; after that, more than likely, she's not.

-Don't ask her what movie too she wishes to see or where she hopes to have dinner.

Take control and decide for both of you. Women desire you to take control and lead the interactions. Don't be 'wishy-washy' and indecisive!

Don't go extremely out of your way to do things for her. Act to her as you 'd act to a friend about favors. Treat her as an individual.

Do not hesitate to rip their clothing off, bend them over a chair &pound the crap out of them often. On a subconscious degree, all females like to be dominated by a reliable person-- just as long as she is saved with him. Women might be the fairer sex, but they are not made from glass as long as it is done in a method which she enjoys and is pleasing for her.

Dos:

-Do act with confidence in any circumstance, especially if you're not especially outstanding looking. Otherwise, you are sunk from the start.

You can move on many ladders that you might not come across in the past. That being said, you need to get her focus at first. All that's required is confidence and being comfortable in your very own skin.

Pre-planned lines nearly never work. A simple "Hi," will work as long as she likes you.

-Do be busy with other things in life, whether that is family friends, working, doing pastimes, or dating different other ladies. Women want to see that you are the kind of person that is in need, whether it be from various other women, companies, or friends. Likewise, if you need to make shit, that's better than being always readily available.

Supply & demand idea, similar to basic service economics. She won't like chasing you if you are often chasing her. Give her the present of missing you.

-Do pleasantly reduce to make boyfriends things with her till after you are barely hooking-up and dating. This recommends at least full-make-out sessions. Not holding hands, cuddling, or pecks on the lips. She will attempt to regulate the framework early on and have you jumping through her hoops. Managing the frame is essential.

-Do learn to be watchful for the little things that reveal enthusiasm. She isn't going to jump on you and tongue tussle you show her interest.

Instead, she'll stay longer than essential when talking with you, she'll poke fun at unexpected jokes, she'll play with her hair, lean or angle herself in the direction of you, and playfully strike you or touch your arm.

-Do tell her only 1/3 of the shit that you plan to say to her. Ask her flexible queries & after that, shut your mouth and let her yell on. When she asks you questions, be funny/witty, and keep your actions shorter. The only solution maybe 1/2 of the question she asked. This is how you stay, "magical.".

Do always remember that there are different other women out there, just as appealing, captivating, and fresh as the one you're having now if you aren't satisfied by taking care of her (either she isn't giving or being demanding), after that by all means just leave and find another woman who will provide you with less issues.

-Do show your feeling with actions, not words—this related to what we examined earlier. Do not share your opinions vocally when any type of woman friends or member of the family asks you to "tell her simply how you feel." If you never plan to see her when more? After that, go right ahead.

What females state they want (a guy that reveals his experiences) and likewise what.

She responds to are two different things. Expressing your feelings for her will transform her off as fast as a light switch.

Do magnify physically when you seem like it. Not when you believe she looks like it. Like we said, "she's not made from a glass," and you need to show her you are physically generated to her. Be lively, be specific, and go for it!

CHAPTER FIVE

Crucial Flirting Tips for Men

The majority of men out there deal with the one big issue that they are not able to flirt with women. Because they do not understand how to flirt with women, lots of songs are frustrated. And it is a significant reason why they're single. Well, here is a set of vital flirting tips for men. Use these tips to bring in women and fill up your solitude.

Do you know flirting is everything about giving - not to get. What are the things you need to 'GIVE' women to 'GET' something from them? Well, is this question too hard? Think once again. You have to give what they have to get what you need. Women like compliment and care; they want to be treated like women. This is the essential flirting advice for men, simply give women these two things, and you will have lots of women to flirt.

Many women want somebody to lead them in their lives.

They want someone to lead them to make decisions. And it's just a woman nature. If you're asking how to flirt with women, then you should establish an ability to lead women on their ways.

Touch a woman as you're her friend - When you have developed a little intimacy with a woman, then you can increase that intimacy by touching her. You're closer to feel her feelings if you physically touch her. So, you should contact her in natural manners frequently. When you lead her, the best timing to affect a woman materially and create emotional attraction is. When she is about to make a big decision, hold her hands.

Hold her hand when you lead her through a crowd. Now you will get her mentally hooked on you. Congratulations.

You require to know the whole flirting technique to use these tips to a useful life. And once you know how to flirt with women, you'll get on your method to draw in a lot of women to seduce.

Flirting Tips You Can Use Today to Attract Women

Have you ever seemed like the topic of flirting seems to be a total mystery to you? Have you felt like you have no idea and unaware of what makes a woman brought in to you? Don't be discouraged as you are not alone if you think this way. Because it is not something that we have been encouraged to do, the majority of men are not that good when it comes to the art of flirting.

So how can you start discovering how to flirt with women to get them drawn into you? Here are tips you can use to help you get going today:

1. Tease her

Teasing is among the most effective techniques when it comes to flirting with women, but it is also probably among the most overlooked methods. A lot of men try to show their interest to the woman they like by showering her with compliments, compliments, and more compliments. Think about how uninteresting this is to a beautiful woman who has been listening to comparable remarks for their whole life? It will show that you are a man of high social value and yet still show to them that you are interested in them if you use a teasing approach instead.

2. Touching her playfully

Without a doubt, the most direct and best way to communicate interest in anybody is through touch. The problem with this is that most men are not comfy with this because they have been taught when they were young that sexuality is the only kind of intimacy that is appropriate for a man. Just take a look at how hardly ever men hug each other as compared to women, and you will get what I mean.

3. Facial expressions

A lot of men have been told to smile more as a way of flirting with women. Smiling too much can, in some cases, backfire and make you come off as clingy and a "great man" what you need to instead mix your smiles with subtle expressions such as laughs, playful winks, narrowing of the eyes, or any other emotions that express some kind of inner thought. This leaves the woman trying to think about what you truly mean, and it can genuinely help to stimulate some interest!

4. Subtle sexuality

Don't let the cultural stereotypes from the media and your environment fool you. There is no doubt that women love sex as much as men do, but they are probably only not comfortable with saying it out due to stereotypes. But if you can discuss it subtly and leave her thinking, you can be sure that she won't stop thinking about you.

There are lots of men who never learn how to flirt with women very well. They look and sound ridiculous, striking up a woman with a corny line or, at best, "Can I buy you a drink?" It's no surprise that a lot of men feel awkward and clueless when it comes to drawing women's attention.

Do you need to know how to flirt with women? Are you truly tired of being rejected because you're approaching them the same way every other man they fulfill is approaching them? Making and smiling eye contact may make her a little less anxious that you're not an ax murderer, but it isn't going to make you stick out in the crowd. It's like many sheep standing around the bar, bleating. What you truly need is these little-known tips to bring in women by flirting. Not only will they be less ridiculous-sounding, but women will also notice them and you a breath of fresh air.

-No More Mr. Nice Guy

It's challenging to flirt with women and have success until you have at least an idea as to how attraction works for them. Women are drawn to men who make them feel safe and a little intrigued at the same time. They don't want men who bend backward to please them at every turn. You're going to end up with a considerable chiropractic doctor's expense and no date if you're the latter.

Think about this: Would you feel secure in the company of someone who did whatever you desired them to do, precisely the way you wanted it done, without ever questioning you or thinking for themselves. One would hope not! Of course, it's accessible to boss around that kind of person, but you'll be tired to tears in no time. Women can identify a spineless jellyfish very quickly. Women desire manly men, not pushovers. If you are always 100 percent acceptable and obedient to her every impulse, she'll soon realize you don't have any self-esteem. He can be badgered, not only by her but by everybody.

This goes against most of what you've been taught about women, but stop being Mr. Nice Guy 24/7. This is probably one of the essential tips for dating you will ever learn. Find out to jeopardize, but not all the time. Often, things need to go the way YOU desire them to go.

Other Tips

Be Unpredictable

If you want a woman to feel safe and secure, how is it possible to create a balance between security and a bit of conspiracy? You don't want to bore her to tears by being a doormat, but you don't want to be viewed as an overbearing jerk, either. The best way to achieve this is to include a little unpredictability occasionally, and a touch of mystery. Leave her guessing for a bit. It is essential to balance this out with duty and self-confidence.

The best way to achieve this is to keep your life, your character, and your worths simply as they are, even if they aren't accurately made to her orders. You may lose some due to this, but you may also be amazed at how much more some women will want you when they realize your desire can't control you.

You're not the only guy contending for the attention of a lovely woman, which means she's now in the habit of having men leap when she snaps her fingers so that they can keep her attention. Women can get bored with this constant pandering, so if you genuinely want her attention, let her know in little ways that while you 'd be pleased to be part of her life, you also have a mind of your own, and you intend to use it. This will set you apart from the rest of the flock of sheep following her, bleating. A little bit of unpredictability can be an excellent thing.

What, you ask, is the final dating signal?

When She Tests You, teasing Her

Now you understand that women end up being tired with a man who does exactly what they want when they want, you're asking why a lot of women want their men to leap when they whistle. It's quite simple: She's evaluating to see if a man is brave enough to walk up to her, or if he's merely cowardly—the majority of men who fail this test end up in the "just friends" classification.

It's easy to determine these tests. Most times, they are completely unreasonable or ridiculous. The best way to "pass this kind of analysis is to tease her gently for being silly. Doing this automatically brings you to the head of the class.

Using these guidelines will make it possible for you to take pleasure in a substantial distinction in your dating life. Your male friends will be lining up to ask you what in the world you're doing differently because unexpectedly, you'll be the one who known how to flirt with women.

Tips of Flirting with Body Language

Flirting isn't bad, particularly if you understand how to do it right. When you flirt, and you'll be pleased to realize that people like it when someone is doing the flirts with them, it is quite hot. It is a way of regarding individuals; it has something to do with smiling, whispering, and touching. As soon as you do it best and in the right environments, it is a potent tool to attract the attention of your date. Do it in the wrong situation; you'll be declined.

Here are some ways to flirt using eye contact:

o Pupils can be dilated while attempting to preserve eye contact

o Eye contact together with arched eye eyebrow looks attractive

o Fast eye motion with a blinking

o Any type of winking

o Eye contact by which the gaze is held longer than the usual occasion.

Here is somebody language that means flirting:

o Thrusting the chest outwards while at the same time holding your gaze to your date.

o Mirroring or the copying of gestures that your partner would do

o Holding your stare while at the same time doing the rhythm of the music o Having the legs crossed towards your date

o Display of flesh arm

You can do these things discussed above, but it is essential to understand the willingness of your appointment. When you flirt, then you better stop so you will not turn her off, in case he does not like it. You need to see the signs just to be sure.

How to Flirt With Women - Flirting Tips for Shy Guys

Among the most challenging things for a guy to the divine is when a woman is interested. Women are more careful than men and wait a while to indicate that there is potentially some interest. Read those words thoroughly - possibly some interest. Women usually don't leap into things. So how do you understand when to pursue?

Generally, men have been the aggressor, but I can assure you that is not always the very best technique. Sure, be aggressive, but do it gently, and be ready to back off if you want to have success. Lots of women will simply shut you out if you persist when they have not shown some interest, or have made it clear that they are not interested.

How to Flirt With Women-Flirting Tips for Shy Guys

-Cultivate a Confidant - One right approach is to expect negatives in conversation. If, during your getting-to-know-you discussion, there are many topics that you think differently, then perhaps you will be friends and not "intimate" friends. If you know of an approaching instance that she may like, do it and wait on a response. Now, there is an idea - remain on an answer. This can likewise be a way of learning some things she does not like.

A good thing to remember is that a long-term relationship is based on relationships, not just desire. There is absolutely nothing incorrect with lust-- without it, a number of us would not be here. You must keep in mind that your woman buddy, considerable other, enthusiast, whatever, will be a pal and confidant as well as all the other excellent things. You need to have the ability to slam each other, share tricks, share good things, and evil. Somebody once said that a good friend is somebody whose faults you understand and you love them anyhow. That is not to state that every single thing needs to be shared. Who among us does not have a skeleton or two? Beware what you share-- it will not always be a good idea. Besides, why would you want to reveal something hurtful? Simply be honest in all things, and then you don't have to fret.

-Don't Be a Sore Loser

As men, you should realize that women are not always interested even if they are interested. This harkens back to the principle of dealing with women with equanimity. The most desirable and beautiful woman may just not have an interest in you. It does not necessarily mean there is anything wrong with you-- she may like a different kind of male. I have heard a lot of men compete that a certain woman is "foolish" because she did not give him a tumble. Well, just think of that and examine who is being dumb. The thing to do is to be friendly with her, and keep your eye peeled for someone else who might be thinking about you. Never annoy the woman who rejected you.

At the end of the day, if a woman is keen on you, she will find a way to let you know. Things will happen if you are smart enough to see the sign and act on it. If you are not, it's your loss. So keep your eyes open and your brain in equipment. Be open to all possibilities and be ready to act upon them. Don't push yourself on anyone, especially women!

Tried And Tested Tips On How To Flirt With Women And Get Sexual

You have approached her. You've talked for sometimes, and it's clear that she's enjoying it. Even better, she's comfortable with you.

What are you going to do next?

Well, guess what: it's time for flirting and stepping things up as far as sexuality is concerned. After all, the reason why you approached her is to get to know her "within and out." This is something that the average chump disregards.

They don't escalate and get stuck. All they could get is that minor peck on the chick. And when he tries to advance (way too late now), the girl responds: "Let's just be a friend. I believe we're better off that way."

You sure don't want that, do you? If you are struggling, if you don't know how to flirt with women and make her feel comfortable in your sexuality, the following tips ought to get you started in the right orders.

- How To Flirt With Women Tip 1

Before anything else, you need to have this mindset: speaking about sex is typical; it's cool! People do it daily. Making love and talking about it is similar to speaking about the weather—nothing fancy, nothing complicated, and absolutely nothing to be worried about.

- How To Flirt With Women Tip 2

Drop sexual overtones. Tease her a lot! Twist what she says and accuse her of attempting to seduce you. This needs to be carried out appropriately and excellently. Keep it enjoyable and light-hearted, that's what flirting with a girl is all about.

- How To Flirt With Women Tip 3

Discuss the future. This is among the techniques I love the most! By talking about a future event where you and she would be making love, you are not just implanting that idea into her head. You are enhancing the idea that you, together with doing the 'deed' is just a matter of time.

- How To Flirt With Women Tip 4

Be detailed, be very descriptive! This one is a little bit advanced. Likewise, you need to make sure that your babe is comfortable with your sexuality. By being detailed, you are developing a comprehensive and very sensual vision of you and her getting on it.

How to Flirt With Women - Tips to Ensure You Will Never Be Lonely

Are you one of those people who just does not know how to flirt with women? Are your attempts at flirting consulted with tepid interest at the very maximum, but more frequently with straight-out rejection? You have to do something to cure the situation immediately else you will end up lonely and depressed. It is an outright misconception that you can do nothing to improve your social abilities, and particularly ones that will help you interact with the opposite sex. You don't even need to be vibrant or good looking to be successful with women as long as you know how to talk with them quite well.

Flirting with women is an art, and you can find out the fundamentals of it. You can do much better than that and become truly successful in your interactions with women as long as you have the right training on how to flirt with women.

When they try to flirt, lots of men are too rigid. There is very limited opportunity for this succeeding because many women find this kind of habit very off-putting. What you need to be able to represent is an image of self-esteem, but need not stumble on as big-headed or pushy. You must also be as natural as possible because there is plenty of fish out in the sea and you will find more than one woman who wishes to be with a man like you. You are not likely to appear worried or required if you just be your natural self, and this is something that the opposite sex will find lovely. The confidence you obtain from having this knowledge will make you more adventurous and attractive.

Flirting is more about having a fantastic discussion rather than attempting to pressurize a woman to go out with you. Since this will make you very interesting to the women you meet, you need to develop the skill of being an excellent listener. They will be extremely grateful to open up to you, and you will get lots of chances to ask them out. This does not mean that you need to sit there silently. When the time comes, practice all kinds of vital things to say so that you are ready. Make sure that you get all possible information on how to flirt with women so that you can talk with any attractive woman you see without worrying about rejection.

Three Closely Guarded Techniques on How to Flirt with Women Revealed!

If you want to be active with lovely women, understanding how to flirt with women is vital. Women love flirting with men who know what they're doing. So if your flirting skills include saying "Hello there," and nothing more, you need some assistance. If you take note of the three carefully secured methods, you're going to enjoy more success with women than you're presently having.

1. Become A Bad Boy

Forget about being a good man. Bad boys are where it's at. Women love bad boys, even though they may state they're looking for a good guy. Often women report something but do the overall reverse. If you're not sure about what a woman is saying, look carefully at her actions.

Women love enjoyment, secret, and romance in their lives and think that bad boys can perform. They likewise wish to feel safe when they're out on a date with a guy. Since bad boys have credibility for being their man, a woman will feel safe when she's out with a bad young boy.

The last person, a woman, wishes to date is a wimp. Sadly, sometimes women correspond nice guys with sissies. So if you want to understand how to flirt with women, try to be more of a bad boy.

2. Excite Her With Your Unpredictability

This tip advances from being a bad kid. Women love the unpredictability, along with enjoyment and romance. Make her wonder if you're going to request for her phone number when you first meet her - your method may work so well that she'll end up asking for your number instead!

Being unforeseeable does not mean standing her up at the last minute, however.

3. When You Flirt, have Fun

A lot of men deal with flirting as a chore - and after that wonder why they're not active with women! If you need to know how to flirt with women, then you need to take pleasure in the actual practice.

Have a good time speaking to her and ensure you enter her private area - not so close that she can smell your breath, but near enough, so you can connect and touch her jewelry or her bag. Enjoyable, flirty movements like these are essential to a successful flirting method.

If you include the previous tips into your flirting efforts, you're sure to get a better reaction than if you follow what you're already doing (which isn't working).

These three carefully protected methods have just shown you how to flirt with women. If your techniques aren't working, why not try these instead? All you are required to do is get out there and practice till they end up being a force of habit. Accept your inner bad boy, end up being unpredictable, and enjoy flirting with beautiful women. Pretty soon, you're going to be among those cool people who understand how to flirt with women!

CHAPTER SIX

Why Flirting and Other are Related Matters

Flirting and fun are carefully associated. Since flirting, when specified loosely, merely implies fun and intriguing way of telling somebody you like that you are interested in them, this is. When you get into a room filled with people, and you barely know anyone there, you may be bored, especially if you are not the flirting type. However, if you like, you can flirt the entire evening with people you barely know without it turning into something simple. If you get to talking to some of the people you were flirting within the room and you feel that you liked them, you can tease yourself to a first date and maybe a long and delighted relationship. Relationships I will always firmly insist are begun with flirts.

Flirting and body movement is also quite judiciously related. Many people will always start flirting with somebody they hardly know by giving one body movement. The body languages I am talking about are the eyes, eye eyebrows, the mouth, the legs, and the hair. An individual will see a person in a gathering, and the first body movement they are going to send is going to be the eyes. They will look at them and smile that way; the person will get the info that the person wants to be familiar with them a little. They can retaliate with a sign of their own if they like them. Another flirting gesture that is going to be used by the woman is that of playing with their hair. If a woman likes you, she is going to play with her hair. Flipping it every long shot, she gets to show it off. A woman's hair is her priced belongings, and by having fun with it, she understands for sure that you will discover and see that she is a fun person to be with.

Flirting and jealousy are also slightly related, particularly in partners. This is because given that flirting is so much enjoyable, people who are in relationships do not wish to be left. This does not mean that individuals they are in relationships with will understand that they are flirting harmlessly, and they do not mean any damage to come to their method. Whenever a partner notices the other flirting with someone of the opposite sex, they get so envious. They can not say why they are flirting while they are in a relationship. When you want to start flirting, ensure that your partner is agreeable to the idea of you flirting with somebody else. Converse that it does not mean anything which could improve the relationship between the two of you.

Flirting and self-confidence are also closely related. A confident individual goes a long way in attaining something. Flirting has been known to increase a person's confidence by a very significant portion. Those people who are shy are motivated to flirt because it will boost their confidence. Flirting has likewise been related to enhancing people's relationship and sex life.

How to Use Conversation to Establish a Deep Connection with Her

Here are some of the most persuasive psychological topics you'll wish to go to when producing a deep emotional connection with a woman you're having a conversation with.

CONNECTING TOPIC # 1: EXPERIENCES

Our experiences are deeply tied to feeling. Whether youth, travel experiences, quitting a job and pursuing a risky new professional course, or anything of the type, our experiences are tied to emotions.

Here are some examples of methods you can get her to open about some of her experiences:

" What was it that made you desire to move to this city?" "What huge experiences have you been on?"

" What's the most interesting place you've traveled to?"

Talking to her about experiences she's had frequently cause amazing stories and stacks of emotion. More importantly than that, diving into the feelings behind her experiences opens up unique ways for you and her to relate to each other.

Here are some relevant examples of ways you might dive more into the feeling behind such experiences:

" How did it feel to do [X]."

" What was it like when you did [X]."

When it comes to associating with her experiences, you need not be scared, not having done the specific same things as her. Once you dive much more in-depth and get her opening up about how she felt about particular experiences, you can relate with her with various skills that triggered you to feel the same feelings.

So, for example, she may say that she stopped her corporate job and became a tour guide on some tropical island. When you dive deeper, she'll most likely reveal that she felt anxious and anxious about whether it 'd be all for the best-- weather she 'd regret it all as a "big mistake" and wish she stuck to her corporate job.

Now, you might not have done anything comparable, but you've probably been in a situation where you've felt similar emotions. For example, you may have moved from another country, began a business, or something of the kind. You can relate to her on an emotional level.

That said, don't endlessly drone on about your experiences. Briefly relate it to an experience you've had in your life (if relevant), and after that, flip the spotlight back on her. This allows her to understand that you "get her" and that you're listening and taking interest-- and that, heck, you guys are sort of comparable in some methods. But at the same time, you avoid being practically silent the whole conversation and having her start doubting that you're even focusing on what she needs to say or that you "get her." going on from the past (experiences), the next emotional subject is based on the present ...

CONNECTING TOPIC # 2: PASSIONS.

What are your passions? What do you love doing?

Scuba diving? Building organizations? Tinkering in the garage? Taking a trip?

Dealing with innovative engineering tasks at work?

Whatever it is, I desire you to think about it for a moment. Seriously. If merely for a 2nd, stop reading and just thinking of whatever it is you love to do.

Now that you've believed about that, how do you feel? How do you think when you consider whatever it is you love to do?

Probably great?

Well, women are no different when they are discussing anything.

It is what they love to do-- their passions-- they associate those positive feelings with being around you.

Here are some examples of ways you can get her discussing her passions:

" What do you love doing?".

" What sort of activities get you truly thrilled?" "What are you incredibly passionate about?".

And, once again, you can naturally dive into the emotions behind her passions.

Here are some examples of how you might do that: "What is it about [X] you love?".

" How do you feel when doing [X]" "Why are you enthusiastic about [X]."

You might find that you can quickly get her talking about her enthusiasm relate (and thus get in touch with her)--particularly if you both love to do the same kinds of things. (Note: Don't pretend you like to do something if you don't, she'll quickly have the ability to tell you're devising, and it'll just come off as extremely clingy, unattractive, and off-putting.), moving from the past (experiences) to the present (enthusiasm), the next psychological topic connects to the future.

CONNECTING TOPIC # 3: ASPIRATIONS.

Her objectives. Her hopes. Her dreams. What does she want to do in life?

People think of their dreams, but seldom get the possibility to speak about.

Because many people don't believe in asking, them, getting her to open up about her aspirations increases a whole bunch of pleasant, confident emotions-- all of which she'll unconsciously relate to you.

Here are some ways you can dive into this topic:

" What are your biggest goals?".

" What kind of things have you always wished to do?" "What are you aiming to achieve this year?".

Here are some ways you can dive into the feelings and emotions, related to her hopes and dreams:

" How would you feel if you did that?".

" What would your life look like if you accomplished that/'.

Carrying on, we've discussed emotional conversation subjects based on past, present, and future. Now, let's take a look at another sensitive topic that's more internal ...

CONNECTING TOPIC # 4: MOTIVATIONS.

Why does she do what she does? What makes her desire what she wants?

What encourages her? The vast bulk of people never dig this deep ...

Here are some questions you can ask to dive into this topic:

" What made you go for that?" (I.e., her college major or profession.)

 "Why do that?" (I.e., what made her do/choose something she did, an excellent question to ask if she's telling you a story, etc.) You can dive even more in-depth with issues such as:

" How do you feel now that you're doing [X]" "What made you want to achieve [X]."

IT'S ALL A BALANCING ACT.

Previously on in this book, you discovered the best techniques for becoming a tempting flirt. In this chapter, you've found how to get in touch with women on a psychological level genuinely maybe the hardest part is neither the flirting nor the linking, but rather balancing the two.

If all you do is flirt, she may enjoy it at that time, but she'll probably end up flaking on you and even just forgetting you completely. There's no connection.

On the other hand, if all you do is have deep conversations and connect emotionally, she'll see you as a "just friends," and you'll end up being her pal, not enthusiast.

Balance the two so you produce both sexual tension and emotional connection.

INTENSIFY, ESCALATE, ESCALATE.

On the interwebs lives a funny little group called "NoFap." As the name implies, these are men that avoid porn, masturbation, and (self- administered) orgasm. (They refer to this as "PMO" for brief.) These so-called "astronauts" often say that, for some reason, they find themselves being successful more with women.

Imagine you have not orgasmed in days, weeks, or even months. You're going to be a horny mofo, right?

And, when you're connecting with attractive women, you're going to be more aggressive. You're not going to sit around have a respectful discussion only. You're going to attempt (whether knowingly or unknowingly) to take that woman to bed as soon as possible. Their horny nature makes them seduce women faster and more aggressively.

Now, why on earth and I telling you this bizarre story?

Here's why: I don't want you to make the mistake of stopping working from escalating the interaction.

You can flirt with a woman endlessly and speak to her forever about a gazillion emotionally-charged subjects. If you don't aggressively escalate the interaction and get intimate, it will all be for naught.

Lesson: Don't just talk and flirt. Get close or, at the minimum, get her number and set up a time to "get a drink/coffee." Be bold, be quick, be gone. Don't be around forever without escalating the interaction.

Take a Good Flirt Quiz - Do You Enjoy the TheFlavor Of Love?
The flavor of love is to love and be loved back. It is considered as the charm of love. If you love somebody who does not reciprocate your feelings, it is very heartbreaking. How do you tell whether somebody is into you? Does valuing your hairdo enough as a sign that somebody has an interest in you? The level of a relationship between two people will be told by how they flirt. If they flirt a lot, the general public concludes that there true love in their relationship. It is not always that a flirt turns out to be a romantic offer, but if there is an already existing dating relationship, the level of

flirting needs to show the development. This can be done by taking an excellent flirt quiz.

For extra relationship effectiveness, you should have the ability to flirt more. Flirtation draws out the taste of love in many relationships and marriages. Some married people do not acknowledge the power of flirting. Top on the list of a good flirt quiz needs to question your behavior in your spouse's presence. Do you flirt with her more? Or do you use words or just body language flirting towards your spouse? If you flirt all the time to make her feel unique, you may be doing that, but always ensure that the flirt is from genuine observation. An overstated flirtation makes you look insincere and a non-serious enthusiast. If you do not flirt at all, you may be causing your partner to feel unappreciated—some couples do away with flirting as soon as they produce children. The kids should not work as an inhibitor in your being flirtatious.

All the partners need to know that if you do not flirt routinely with your loved one, somebody else somewhere will do that. Because it will be a unique treatment, she/he will react to it. If something romantic is made up, who is to be blamed? When someone else flirts with your girlfriend or partner in your presence, a good flirt quiz ought to question your response. It is a clear sign that you are not a liberated lover if you respond with a lot of hostility. I am not dismissing jealousy, but you must trust your partner to follow you. The incoming flirtation serves to validate your words, and because they will not be new to her ears, she will say something like "thank you" without a lot of excitement or "I am aware." Won't this make you proud? Of course, it will assure you that your partner delights in the real taste of love.

On the other hand, if the response to the question on the flirt quiz on the list is a magnificent smile to acknowledge the appreciation, you are a loving sweetheart or a husband. The taste of love is in knowing that you are appreciated when your spouse ultimately believes in you. It is the best feeling in the whole world. You should have the ability to flirt with another woman in her presence. If somebody is smart and you tell her so, this will make her believe in you too.

CHAPTER SEVEN

Your Approach

This the only way to change things

Okay, possibly that tail end was a little extreme on you. In some cases, reality needs to bite a bit, though, to enact change. However, I don't wish you to start unfavorable self-talk or feel rotten about the state of current affairs. The purpose of this book is not to make you feel dreadful or like you did something wrong. It's for you to find out and learn from previous mistakes. It's just currently you might not even know that you were doing things wrong. Maybe its that you don't even recognize where your game is entirely breaking down? Or perhaps you have been your own harshest critic, and it's not as bad as you think. However, you chose out this book for a reason, so it's time to break things down much more and get real with yourself.

Uncertain of how to do that? Feel unpredictable when it comes to finding out what you even need to be real about? However, if you tried honestly making a note of the qualities you desire from a future partner, then you have made a good start! Now we will try examining, in a little bit more detail, the next step in mastering the art of flirting-- The Approach.

I can remember reflecting on what my approach resembled. I winced thinking about how I froze and how I had such a tough time, even speaking with a woman. Not only that, but when I did get up the nerve to approach women, I found that I didn't have the first hint about how to speak with her or what to discuss. In hindsight, I was going after the entirely wrong woman for me because I hadn't taken note of what I wanted. I felt down and out like I would never get better at this whole dating thing.

At that time, though, I recognized that I needed to be sincere with myself, and I was. I got hard on myself in the sense that I wished to grow, and I decided that this was the time to do it.

Taking Responsibility For Your Life-- Stop TheExcuses!

All set to start getting real? This is where you stop getting in your way. This is where you take responsibility for your life. Own it like a real guy. You will have to stop justifying or making reasons or validating things as being the outcome of outdoor elements. You probably don't think that you're guilty of this, but we've all done it in the past. This simply might be the type of habits that is keeping you from getting what you truly want-- women !!!

If You Give Into The Excuses, Then You Are Only Hurting YourselfHarming

Let's start with a little sincerity and stock here and look at what has caused you to get to where you are. Sure, a lot of us aren't just good at talking to women, though with practice and the right skills, this can be changed. Admittedly, it can be a very intimidating thing, and we struggle to figure out just what we're supposed to say. I have sat where you are right now and felt that seclusion and aggravation, but you don't have to give in to that anymore. Discussion is hard enough, so flirting is like it's a world away.

The Skills To Interact Successfully.

Believe about what happens from the time you approach a woman to the time she turns you down.

Since you have to break down the whole interaction, this is where it all gets real. Since this is the only way you are going to get much better, don't fear it but face it. Think about what goes on from the minute that you attempt to speak with her. Do you even attempt to approach her, or do you simply put that off? When you are talking to her, are you trying to overcompensate or be someone that you think you should be? Do you become a bumbling idiot? If it's always her fault or just "not the best time," then you know that you have some reasons to deal with it. Yeah, I know no one wants to take the blame off of someone else and put it on themselves; however, it has to be done.

What would you change that you think might make a distinction with women?

Believe about the encounter as a whole and believe about what you may be blamed for the wrong reasons:

If you're sincere, you can typically cut through the clutter to see what kind of excuses you keep going to. These are the things that are holding you back! These are likely contributing factors if you are always blaming the woman or the timing or whatever else. If you simply sit it out because you make sure that she's going to say no, then you are shooting yourself down before you even get an opportunity.

If you are blaming other men for "taking" the hot girl that you saw first, that's another reason. If there are things that you can point to every single time which you make sure are to blame for you not getting the woman, then you need to give up the blame game and rise to your responsibility! Excuses won't take you anywhere, but they will stop you from getting what you desire, so do away with them.

What are you genuinely looking for in a woman? Be truthful here too, and go beyond just "a hot one."

What do you think that a woman like that is interested in?

How can you be a man that women are drawn in to and thinking about?

How can you stand out from the crowd and win women over?

What does flirting mean to you, and how can you get much better at it? How do you think that flirting can help you to win a woman over?

Yeah, I understand it's a lot of questions, and you don't have to answer all of them. The only thing is, though, that if you want to change your approach and your result, you need to analyze what has been happening. Being truthful with yourself is the only way to get to the heart of the woman.

I dealt with it too once you reveal the roadway obstructs and the problems that have been holding you back, then you can get to the beautiful things. There's some excellent stuff too-- think of the thrill of experiencing a successful flirt! Nothing improves your ego and confidence rather than it. You will astonish yourself at how your approach can take shape and how you get the girl—all that by being truthful with yourself and making an effort to look at what has been happening. Yup, the best is yet to come!

Take Note:

- Stop blaming women and other reasons. You are responsible just to yourself.

- Analyzing your unfavorable and favorable techniques to women from the past will assist you in determining what works and what doesn't work in your approach to women.

- Moving forward, when you have discovered the answers, you can develop a plan to overcome the negative and positives of your flirting approach.

The Proper Way and Time To Approach and Make Your Move.

Oh, for the love of God, will you please stop waiting for the right time? Will you stop assuming that this resembles some motion picture where the music is playing in the background as you slowly approach each other, delighting in incredible love at first sight? I'm not saying that it's not possible, I'm just saying that it's not possible. If you continue to waste your life waiting for that perfect moment or that best situation to come, then you are going to be waiting for an extended period and miss many opportunities. Yes, even men can get caught up in the idea of a perfect scenario to meet their dream woman, but you need to come down to earth here, my friend!

You can give yourself a million excuses for why you don't wish to approach her today. It may be that you aren't feeling on top of your game. You might tell yourself that you are sick of rejection. Maybe you just feel like "hanging with your boys," or it may be that you are okay single. Does any of this sound familiar? Yup, we've all existed since we all desire the stars and the moon to be lined up so that we can approach this woman without being shut down. Sounds excellent in theory? In practice and truth, though, this is just not how it usually works.

Sad but true! Women don't always wait on that one right sign, so why are you doing that to yourself?

I get it, working up the nerve to approach a woman isn't always easy. I comprehend it takes courage, and getting rid of that fear of rejection. However, I do know something, though; opportunities present themselves, and you best be on the lookout for them. If you are so deliberate or worry a lot about rejection, then you are losing out. You need to take dangers sometimes to get them to pay off. You need to be willing to put yourself out there. Just what are you so afraid of in the first place?

You'll never know up until you attempt!

It will pass you by if you don't live in the moment at some point in your life. I know how easy it is to just mix into the wall. I understand what it feels like to offer yourself a million reasons or excuses why you shouldn't talk to her. I know that feeling of merely waiting for the "right time" or telling yourself that it doesn'thave to be today. Stop the madness and start focusing on the essential things that matter.

Start searching for methods to seize the moment, get yourself out there, man up and get some courage, and talk with the woman. You'll never know till you attempt, and I promise you that it will be more comfortable with the practice and be worth it!

Here are a few things to assist you figure out how to get that courage and stop getting in your way, perhaps enjoying and getting dates. Yup, you can do this, and the only one stopping you is yourself. The fact hurts, doesn't it, my friend?

Suck it up, buttercup, and go out there and stop fretting about the rejection that you may or might not experience.

Taking Action!

-Know that the right time doesn't exist: Take an action back and let this one sink in. Yes, you're a smart man, and you want good things to occur, but they don't always come in and grab you by the hand. Lean in, more detailed, come on a little bit better, okay, listen to me very thoroughly, and hear what I'm saying perfection does not exist. Mind-blowing, right? Perfect women, perfect relationships, perfect moments-- none of it, excellent must be taken out of your dictionary.

You have to be happy and find your right match, but she's not going to come in the type of pure excellence. So why would you assume that right occurs any longer than perfect relationships? If you sit there and keep waiting on that best moment, you're going to age alone.

Instead, learn that there is no such thing and that you are just making reasons and excuses for yourself. None of which will lead you to anything good. Forget about that right time you have conjured in your mind and just go for it; you've got this!

-Make your right timing and live in the moment: Okay, let's take this one more action, and let this sink in and savor it. You create your own best timing. You get to live in the moment and experience things. You get the pleasure of making your own decisions and letting them work for you. Living means that you delight in how it feels to experience pleasure and even pain. Profound ideas, huh? If you don't experience great hurt, you will not understand what it feels like. If you go through life being merely on the line of blah, you will never get to feel the enjoyment and excitement of flirting and approaching a woman. Yes, the truth is it won't always work out, but then it wouldn't be interesting if you understood it ever would!

The important thing is that you will never understand till you try and though you presume it will be uncomfortable, it might be the start of something great. So make your own "best" time judiciously. Live in this minute and brush aside all the thoughts working against you, then you can talk to any girl you desire.

It's not a match, but you just never know till you try if it's not a game. Go all out, make this your most extraordinary chance, and tell yourself "what the hell" and go speak with her. Just making that decision puts you in control, helps you to be useful in your own life, and for that reason, suggests that good ideas are actual to come your way!

-Go in looking unrehearsed but with a plan of what to say: Okay, this is all about creating actionable steps? I will assist you with "how" and what to focus on, as well as what to say. You can be a very intriguing and intriguing conversationalist. Think about and maybe make a list of questions or topics that you can use so you can walk up to a woman and speak with her.

It may be that you just look at yourself in the mirror and say, "hey tiger, it's high time!". Act and give yourself a pep talk. Try just to act natural, don't worry so much about what you have practiced saying as happen word for word. Bud, it won't happen that way. It's all about having a basic plan of things to discuss with her. It should be as essential as naturally approaching her and just having a few minutes' conversations.

You will not have the ability to enter and chat her up right off the bat. You will need practice. So simply attempt some table talk with different women without any result intended. When you have practiced this and feel a bit comfier, you can bring in the more flirty elements.

You don't need a master plan with steps to it, however rather only an idea of what you want to say which you want to do this. Yup, it takes courage, but you've got this, and if you decide that you will do it, then you will hold yourself liable—plan on merely saying hi and asking a bit about her. Don't make it a script, instead just a few general ideas on how to make eye contact and talk with the girl once and for all.

Number one thing on your list needs not to bore her! How are you going to avoid that? That's right-- talk about things she wants to speak about. The essential stuff most men think women wish to hear is not the right topics. Put it by doing this;

Theoretical concern: If a girl came near you, having just read a current list of 'male; discussion topics like a computer game, stock trading, weapons, motorcycles, cars and trucks, sports, virtual truth HD goggles, etc. and begins droning about them, more than most likely you will find a few of it fascinating, but many of it will send you off to the land of nod. It's the very same if you try talking about a basic list of stereotypical 'woman' discussion topics. To find out what she likes talking about, just attempt a fundamental question like, "Hey, what sort of things do you like doing most in your extra time? You are a winner if she seems engaged and starts talking about what she wants.

I'm guessing you are asking now, how do I tell whether what I'm speaking about with the girl is right? Well, let me give you an example of interest and not interested.

Not interested in topic:

Guy: Do you ever make your food?

Ann: No, it looks like a beautiful idea, but I don't have the time.

Guy: Ah, right, yeah, it's tough to find time on your own nowadays. When you are free, what do you choose to do with those precious hours?

Ann is saying here that making her food doesn't intrigue her. So think what Guy, that excellent story you were going to inform her about all your homegrown veg in your kitchen is going to bore her to death. Can you see here how Guy managed to save himself? He altered tact and asked her what she does in her extra time.

Interested in topic:

Guy: Have you been anywhere fascinating overseas just recently?

Ann: Oh my gosh, I just got back from the most fantastic trip to Greece. The Castle was breathtaking.

Ann is incredibly enthusiastic about discussing her journey to Greece. Undoubtedly.

The person is on a winning discussion topic here.

The leading pointer here is to frame any questions that you have, so she needs to address in a manner that doesn't make her seem uncool. And this is not to be carried out in a nasty way, merely a subtle and smart way. Take note of the example of Guy's very first subject that didn't interest her; he framed the second question in a manner that made it difficult for her not to give a more in-depth answer. The method he mounted the matter would have made her wish to address something more refreshing and fascinating. If she answered with something vague like, " nothing much actually," she would seem quite lame and boring. Nobody wishes to be viewed as uncool and uninteresting. And to be honest, if a girl is speaking in this manner, then she is tired of talking to you, or she is dull and not the type of woman you want to put effort into trying to get a date from.

Use unclear, dull responses to your questions is a hint to move on, friend!

-Stop letting your worries get in the way and think about the possible results: I desire you to do something about it in a slightly different method here. I want you to take a seat for a minute and analyze what your real fears are. Yeah, I understand, this is asking you to think and dig deep and deal with things you don't always want to deal with. I promise you that it will bring you some clarity. Stay with me now, and let's face this down together. What are your most significant worries here? What is holding you back?

- Are you scared that she will laugh in your face or turn away from you?

- Are you scared that she will decline you before you even get to speak with her?

- Are you afraid that your ego will get bruised with this trial?

- Do you stay away because you just don't know what to say?

- Are you daunted by her and therefore look like a fool?

- Do you simply worry that you will never get the girl, and so you keep making excuses?

Dealing with down the truth isn't always easy, but it's completely worth it. I'm sure that a minimum of one of these reasons or factors is what's holding you back. Do you understand what each of these worries boils down to when you think about it? Embarrassment. I'm betting it with you that even if among the above does not apply when you discover what you're scared of, it will still boil down to fear of shame. If you allow yourself to see what lies in your way truly, then you can shatter that excuse and progress with a purpose to something spectacular. Because you're about to learn how to produce your own, forget about that right time, and after that, you begin to see that being a great conversationalist and using the correct quantity of flirting is well within your reach. Next, we will look at how to handle the fear of shame.

" Don't wait for the perfect moment, take a moment, and make it perfect."

Note well:

- You can prepare, chart, get scientific or even rely on astrology, but the right time to approach a woman does not exist.

- To discover the right one and also increase your opportunity of getting a date, you need to produce and seize as many chances as possible to flirt and converse with women.

- Increase your possibilities of success by knowing there is no best moment; you create your opportunities, make a basic plan of what to do, and conquer related worries.

Easy Ways To Get Over Your Fear About TheApproach

It's okay to be terrified. Being afraid means, you're about to do something actually, courageous.

Okay, yeah, we're men, we're macho, we're huge difficult men, and we're not scared? Sound like a familiar way society sees our sex? You have likely encouraged yourself that you're not afraid of anything, too, if you are sitting there reading this. You probably have stated to yourself, Not me! No other way, I'm not a sissy. I'm a man, and how could I perhaps get scared by the idea of speaking to a woman? Yeah, I understand, so not you at all. Except that it's a large part of the reason you read this book. You may not always think you are terrified of talking to women; however, you are indeed scared of something. Most likely, a worry of emotional discomfort or shame.

Yes, even us guys get frightened, especially when it concerns rejection. And that's ok. We are genuine; we have feelings too! What we need about all else, though, is to seem like we are respected. I've said it before, and I've said it once again, men require regard. Women long for love and love. Men, we crave and need respect. We want and need to feel respected by our peers and the woman that we're interested in. Try as you may, you can't overlook the truth that regards matters much to you. You have to face the reality you are not always going to feel respected in a dangerous situation like flirting. Because she might not be interested, it may not still work out how you think it needs to, and you might end up feeling disrespected by the woman you are talking to.

In a book by Emerson Eggerichs, the best-selling author of Love and Respect, a sample of men were asked: if required to choose between being left alone and unloved worldwide or to be seen as disrespected and insufficient, which would they prefer? 74% of Emerson's male sample answered they would prefer to be left alone and unloved, whereas the reverse is true of the sample taken from women. While this is a little generalization, and to love a woman, you also require to respect her, it highlights how essential feeling respected is to us.

Feeling respected in a relationship is crucial, but it begins with the time that we fulfill a woman. So if that potential regard is compromised or we think that we will not potentially get it, then we are hesitant about carrying out the regard damaging activity. This is specifically true of the approach and could have been among the underlying reasons that you have been reluctant to do it in the past. For that reason, it's more natural to avoid possible confrontation or hurt feelings by avoiding the approach. You know I'm right. Nevertheless, if you equip yourself with this knowledge and can get ready for the risk, it will be less of a blow if you are declined. And yes, regardless of all exceptional laid plans, it will happen occasionally.

If you're prepared to put in the necessary work, you can get rid of barriers and fears!

Don't let your need for respect and the potential hurt to your ego hold you back! Now let's learn those other possible fears about the approach and get some actionable concepts to conquer them. If you have asked yourself the concerns from earlier in this book, you've currently finished part one of this. However, now it's up to you to take it a step further. Now it's up to you to determine how to get rid of that fear.

Here are some of the likely fears holding you back and the action or steps you can attempt to overcome them.

- You worry that she's going to call you out or reject you: Everyone, men or women, frets about rejection. No one likes it. Simply stop for a minute and ask yourself, so what if she declines you? What's actually the worst that could happen if she chuckles in your face (though I highly question she will)? What will happen in the broad picture of your life if she withstands you or turns you away?

It's not going to be a great feeling. Will your ego be briefly bruised? Yes, it will.

Are you going to go to A&E-- NO!

Are you going to be psychologically scarred for life and need a therapist for life-- NO! It's unreasonable to think that she will push you away or laugh you in your face, so learn that. Know that it's much worse in your mind and brush aside those worries in the meantime.

The truth is that you will not die or be severely impaired in the process. So now think about it again-- What is the worst that can take place? You must be able to address something along the lines of this if you have your positive mindset engaged. At worst, I will feel ashamed for about a half-hour at most. If I'm on my own, nobody needs to know. At best, I come with an amusing story to inform my blossoms and have something word over. I can be honest and real with them and potentially even get some tips from one another. They might then feel comfy enough to share and laugh at their chat up fails with me because of my courage.

It's okay to take a look at how previous errors have shaped you and got you to where you are at today, as long as you are taking a look at them to improve yourself. That's positive. You gain from the mistakes and the unfavorable patterns and concerns; however, they must be in the past. I don't care if you have approached 19 women with a negative outcome because you know what? It only might be that out of the 20th woman that you contacted. She might be the one you were meant to meet. You crashed and burned and got hurt in the past-- so what? You felt like crap and got down on yourself, and now it's over. You're Mr. Positivity!

Summon up that courage that you know is deep down in you. Acknowledge that the only way to conquer you fear to put your plan into action, resolve the past hurt, and leave it there. Move on with purpose. If you enable yourself to experience them, I guarantee you that remarkable things await you.

Getting harmed in relationships becomes part of life. You can't experience love without hurt. Know that it won't take place every single time you talk to a woman or get into a relationship. Brush yourself off and go out there again, my friend. I promise good things will come your way if you attempt to talk to women. You can't die from hurt or shame even if you do crash and burn again. Attempt it and see what works for you.

CHAPTER EIGHT

The Body Language You Must Know if you want to Succeed with Flirting

If You Want TO succeed, the Body Language You Must Know

Read her body movement and search for cues, both favorable and unfavorable: Okay, directly, you will not figure this one out right now. Attempting to read women isn't always simple, and you may look like you need a foreign translator. Which, naturally, you kind of do because it can seem like women are in some cases from a different planet. However, I will help you figure this one out.

Did you know that regardless of it always appearing like it is us men that need to approach to start flirting with women, that 90% of the time it is her? If she is pleased with you approaching her, she will be using motions to propose. This is frequently through face, body, and eye signals sent to the targeted guy. You will more than likely have a hugely successful approach if you are observant enough to pick up on these signals. Now, don't go getting too thrilled by this because most men are not extremely great at detecting female body language. We have so much testosterone floating around our bodies that it can trigger us to often mistaken a friendly smile from sexual interest. What a problem!

If you find out to keep an eye for the hints, a lot of body language is subconscious, and she will be giving tricks from left to right and center. Body language is such a colossal place that an entire book might be committed to it. My suggestion is if you want to know more comprehensive details, to complete your further research.

-Eye Contact: A woman who might be interested in, you will usually look your way, capture your eye for a few seconds, and avert again. Check first your zipper isn't down, and you don't have spaghetti sauce splattered down your shirt as the thing she is looking at. She will repeat this glance up to three times if you are great. Inconsistently looking at you and once again, she has actually proposed her interest in your approach.

-Smiling: All you may get is a fast half-smile. Don't rely on merely a quick smile to show approach. Ensure her other signals show the same.

-Posture: If she wants you to approach, her stance will be set to flaunt. By this, I mean she will be correcting the alignment of clothes, touching or snapping her hair, and perhaps gently licking her lips. If she is sitting down, more than likely, she will be sitting straight-backed with legs crossed, displaying whatever she feels are her best assets. Similarly, if she is standing, she might highlight her curves by tilting her hips a little forward. Remember, with a lot of women, this is subconscious and not what they believe is outright and blatant flirting. Don't go up to her if she is displaying this type of body language, believing she is simple and can be treated. You don't want her to have her impression of you as a sleaze, because you read body movement the wrong way!

-Talking with her: If you are making a great impression after approaching her, she might try to find an opportunity to touch you mistakenly. She may repeat the touch to see how comfy you were with it. Here are some favorable facial gestures to watch out for when speaking to her to boost your self-confidence that your first impression and approach are working out.

- o Raised eyebrows: When integrated with a nod or a smile, it usually indicates she is interested and concurring with what you are saying or doing.
- o Active eyelids: It's one of the earliest stereotypical female flirts; however, if she is batting her eyelashes at you, she is flirting back.
- o Dilated students: this only works in a bright setting. Both boy and girl's pupils dilate (get more extensive and darker) if they are speaking with somebody they are interested in.
- o Flared nostrils: This is an involuntary response that happens in females if they are aroused or delighted.
- o Lips: Chewing or licking her lips draws your attention towards them, which is a sexual or arousing part of her body.

The things to be cautious of as hints she is not interested in or has changed her mind about you are noted below.

-Crossed arms: If she has passed her arms, chances are she has withdrawn or bored. She is putting a barrier between you both, and you may need to give up trying to flirt and speak.

-Touching her hair in fast jerky movements: Touching hair in slow mild twisting or twirling is a fantastic sign. However, if it's being done in quick, jerky motions, then this means she is uneasy, ashamed, or bored.

-Looking away: When she is interested in you, she will reveal this by looking directly into your eyes. You've lost her if she is looking at everything, but you then its time to give up.

Women can tell you a lot about their interest in you without ever saying a word. Be on the lookout for cues and discover how to produce your own to make this work to your benefit. Not just do you want to learn how to read her, but you also want to work to make your terrific impression. This originates from learning to read body language and likewise build yourself to win her over and show that you are in tune with these things. Remember that this is just a general guide, and not all women have the same body movement. Likewise, sexual gestures like licking lips are carried out unconsciously; allure is the brain's natural reaction if you are interested in somebody of the opposite sex. It does not instantly mean she wishes to make love with you.

Reading her body movement is an excellent tool for you, but remember, she might be doing the very same, so it is essential for you likewise to give the best cues to start flirting and develop a fantastic impression.

Here's a couple of quick tips.

Smile: What have you got to lose in a fast smile? Even if she turns not to be interested, you will have most likely brightened her day. Smiling always makes you feel more favorable and positive.

Upper body: We keep our chest up, and shoulders pointed towards the most crucial thing in the place. So puff it up and keep it in her direction.

Stance: To make yourself look effective, which is sexy to a lot of women, stand with your feet set broad apart and in her direction. You can likewise put your hands on your hips to create a moving image. Practice this in the mirror because you don't want it to be looking dorky.

Touch: She would like to know you are interested too. So if things are going well and you have started discussing, make a thing of flirting by lightly touching her lower back, arm, or waist. She is probably comfortable with this if she leans in. If not, cease from moving her again till she shows further interest. Girls don't like wandering, creepy hands, so do this with care.

Think about how you desire people to perceive you and the positives that these adds and after that promote it. By this understanding, I mean, do you want to stumble on as the amusing guy; the impeccably dressed guy; the mannered gentleman guy; the outdoorsy guy; the sensitive guy; the quite listening person; the loud outbound person; and so on. Remember, you still need to be yourself, so don't attempt to be the guy you aren't. Work on pressing the angle of your personality that is your selling indicate women in your impression. Put in the work so that someone can't help but go with a good idea of you.

For example, you may now know that you have been trying to put across the funny outbound man in very first impressions, which's not you and what you are comfortable with presenting to women. They will pick this fakeness and get the idea of you as a try-hard. Possibly, you have now listened to the info in previous chapters and taken stock and understand that you are a quiet listener, who is much better at asking interesting questions from the woman they have met. You can now work towards making this the primary thing you will present as favorable in your first impression to women if this is you.

All these features being simple, vulnerable, and sincere, and then putting in the effort to improve it. While you may not like where you are right now, you must be more than ready to give it up.

Be sincere in your assessment and be ready to fix the important things that aren't working for you: If you do think of it, you probably know what isn't working for you. It may be quite apparent, and you never wanted to repair it. You might have felt too overwhelmed to attempt to change up what you knew wasn't favorable for you. Whatever the case might be, sincerity will serve you well here.

I knew that back then, I was not the finest conversationalist, but I faced that down and worked on it. I even became a naturally funnier guy by becoming more at ease in my conversations with women. You can continue to go through life with blinders on, but how is that exercising for you? Be honest in what's not working for you and then put in the work. Enhance the essential things that are creating a tainted or less than a beneficial perception of you. If you can alter that, then you can do anything - and your dating life and first impressions will be favorable from here!

Take note

- First impressions are delicate to get right and need hard work.

- Analyze the type of feeling you are presently making by analyzing past encounters.

To improve or change the type of the first impression you are producing try: getting into their shoes; asking questions to create conversation; reading body movement; figuring out the kind of the first impression you wish to give; being truthful in what need repaired and produce a plan to do it.

Attractive Body Language

As you're reading a book on flirting and talking with women, you most likely wish to have better the ability to draw in women.

Perhaps women seem to dislike you as soon as you open your mouth, maybe you have no clue how to flirt, or maybe you're susceptible to awkwardness.

Whatever the reason, none of that matters if you don't have your nonverbals down pat. You can be the most excellent conversationalist in the world, the world's most practiced flirt, but if you have unsightly body language, you'll be known as scary.

Research studies show that body language has a direct effect on your state of mind, meaning that you can "fool" yourself into feeling incredibly positive, making approaching attractive women a little simpler for you.

Anyhow, let's have a look at how to have women thinking you're a sexy mofo before you open your mouth, as well as how to use nonverbal interaction to make you're flirting more seductive.

BODY MOVEMENT BASICS

" Fie, fie upon her!

There's language in her eye, her cheek, her lip, Nay, her foot speaks; her wanton spirits watch out At every joint and motive of her body."

-- William Shakespeare

Imagine an appealing woman. Picture her sitting with her legs spread large apart ("manspreading," if you will). Envision her also having her hands gripped behind her head, elbows pointing outward. She likewise speaks in a rough, deep, manly voice.

Not so appealing any longer? Why is that?

Men are drawn into feminine women. The woman described above is showing extremely masculine body movement, which we are hardwired to discover unsettling at the best and highly unattractive at worst. Instead, men would find gentle body movement to be more attractive.

Womanly women are drawn into masculine men. They intuitively discover masculine body movement feminine and appealing body movement unsightly.

When you sit with a leg crossed over the knee (like a woman), speak in a high-pitched voice, quickly dart your eyes downward instead of holding eye contact, walk-in fast little actions, and so on, women find that unappealing. Men with feminine body movements are to women what a big, hairy, muscled, deep-voiced lady would be to us men. That is, sexually repulsive.

What does masculine body language look like?

-Expansive.

-Takes more space.

-Terrific posture.

-Slow and purposeful motion (instead of quick, jerky, and unchecked).

-Deep voice (which is done by fully breathing/speaking and unwinding from your tummy, not chest).

-Doesn't smile excessively.

-Swaggers about like a badass. E.t.c.

One of the easiest and essential ways to start embodying the masculine body language is to search for some clips of James Bond and Marlon Brando and use these men as your body movement function models.

Maybe the best method to establish hot, masculine body language is to get a "body language good example" and replicate them. I 'd recommend either James Bond or Marlon Brando (or both!) as great ones to start with.

When flirting, you wish to lean back and demonstrate that you're relaxed and at ease.

No fidgeting. No "pecking"-- continuously leaning in (and back out again) to hear what she's saying, making yourself look like a bird pecking at food.

Instead, make sure your movements are calm and regulated.

By showing robust body movement, you stumble on as (and feel more) confident, helping to make you're flirting more reliable.

Lesson: Have an open, extensive body movement. The most convenient way to do this is to emulate James Bond's body movement. Gentle body movement will, at best, make you extremely unattractive to women (and, at worst, make you sexually repulsive)-- so make sure that your body movement is always manly. You want your body language to put on that of James Bond, not some flamboyant homosexual.

CHAPTER NINE

How To make the Conversation more Friendly

How To Not Make Her Fall Asleep

Most guys (perhaps you included) ask questions like the following:

"What's your job?" "Where are you from?" "What school did you attend?"

Aside from being so dull, they're more potent than sleeping medication; there's one other issue with these questions: They require no more than one word to answer. "Accountant." "Boston." "Hogwarts."

Above that, with enough drinks, she could mistake herself for being in a job interview. So what's the way out?

There are some remedies, so let's start with the easiest

How To Obtain The Most Bang For Your Question

When you ask questions, dive a little deeper. Ask questions that require not a one-word response (or, worse yet, a mere "yes" or "no"), but a more extended, more profound answer. Aim for a paragraph, not one word.

Here's an example:

Guy: Do you like your job?

Girl: Yeah, it's cool.

At least, you get one word ("yes"); at most, you get three.

Not looking good.

Here's an example of how you might tweak it: Guy: Why do you like your job?

Girl: Well, I love...(blah blah blah)

See the difference?

Al.so takes note that women are emotional creatures (as opposed to men who tend to be more logical). Consequently, you can never go wrong, delving into the emotions behind things.

Here's an example of a lost opportunity to establish an emotional connection with the woman:

Girl: I'm a doctor.

Guy: Oh, wow. Long hours?

Here's an example of a guy who seizes the opportunity and establishes an emotional connection:

Girl: I'm a doctor.

Guy: Wow. What's it feel like to save somebody's life?

Yes, the latter example is a little clunky, but you get the idea.

Which question do you think is going to elicit a more emotionally-charged response (to which the guy might be able to relate to an experience in which he felt similarly), create greater emotional intimacy, and get her talking to the guy with powerful, positive emotions? I think the answer's pretty obvious.

Lesson: Ask open-ended questions and, preferably, delve into her emotions and motivations.

Moving on, let's take a look at whether or not you should even be asking questions in the first.

Statement And Question

1. Fuel the conversation- If you think wrongly, she'll always want to know why you guessed what you did. This gives you more to speak about and fuels the discussion.

2. She'll love finding out about herself- There's just one thing women love more than speaking about themselves, which's hearing others talk about her. Whether you guess wrong or right, she'll love hearing about what it has to do with her that made you do what you did.

3. She'll think you're a genius if you guess right- Well, not literally, but she'll be almightily impressed by your perceptiveness.

4. You appear very positive. When you speak in statements, women naturally perceive you to be more dominant, confident, and bold-- all desirable qualities. You look like more of an alpha male.

5. Develops immediate familiarity- When you've just met somebody, you ask each other many concerns. You speak to each other firstly in a statement when you've been good friends (or family) with somebody for years. Thus, by talking to her in speeches, you fool her subconscious into feeling that you two have known each other for long and are more familiar than you are.

6. Gets rid of interview mode- Firstly, you're not asking questions (i.e., "talking to" her) in the first place. Secondly, when you guess aspects of her, that adds more fuel to the fire, giving you non- interview-y things to speak about.

So when it comes to statement versus question, there's no contest.

To give you a clearer image, here are some more examples:

Question: What do you do?

Statement: You look like an artsy type, I wager you're a [some sort of imaginative job]

Question: Want to grab something to eat?

Declaration: You need to be starving; let's get something to eat.

Question: Want to opt for a walk?

Declaration: Let's go for a walk.

Feel the difference? The statements are more active and dominant. On the other hand, the questions sound practically clingy by comparison, as if you're seeking authorization or are unsure of yourself.

Lesson: Turn questions into declarations. You sound significantly more confident, dominant, and competent. Statements can likewise intensify to the discussion in regards to the excitement and having more things to discuss.

From Dull Questions To Flirty Statements

You don't need to stop there, though. So far, we've gone from dull questions to declarations, but if we add a little bit more spice, we can go from blunt questions to speeches, to flirty statements.

Here's an example of concern, statement, and flirty declaration:

Question: What do you do?

Declaration: You look like an artsy type, I wager you're [some sort of imaginative task]

Flirty Statement: Let me guess. you must be a [drug dealer/exotic dancer/astronaut/etc.]".

Now, you don't wish to continually make out-there guesses like "dancer" or "drug dealer," or it'll be using, and you'll come off like a clown. But you can inject a little extra "spice" into your declarations from time to time to give excitement and generate an amusing back and front.

Lesson: You can always weave a completely ridiculous presumption into your declaration to create some enjoyment. You might likewise suggest something sexual to amp up the flirting and produce some sexual stress.

CHAPTER TEN

Playing the Flirting Game

No matter how much wealth you have and who you are, you must follow some tips and rules to flirt with a stunning girl and to make her your own. Yes, occasionally, you might discover a man who has got a lovely woman. You are to think that it happens seldom, or he is nonetheless a lucky man. On the other hand, you would know some men who try their best to get a stunning woman but end up failing. You need to follow an excellent method for attempting to flirt with girls. This is the essential chapter of this book, and it shows you the way to a great date.

Try to Know What Her likings Are

When you are in front of each other, you can not begin flirting with her unless both of you find comfort. Ask her what her favorite subject is, what kind of music interests her, who is her favorite star, and so on. This type of discussion will make your girl feel easy. Unless she opens up to you, you can not begin flirting with her. Try to agree with her preferences and confess that you also have a taste of her tastes. Program some reasoning behind your choices that might impress her. At last, admire her likings.

Keep it secret

You need to ensure that the woman you are flirting with never becomes aware of what is going on. It is better that she does not understand your plan and mission. If she becomes conscious of your intention, you may need to give up the hope of dating and try to find another stunning girl. That is never good news for you. Try to keep it a secret. Another reason for keeping your plan a secret is that you are going to impress her at any expense, and for this, you need to go through a process. If the woman you desired knows your intention for flirting with her, she will take every of your act in before her as a part of your plan. Then impressing her will become next to impossible. So, you should keep it a secret to flirt with her.

Make Her Smile

Try to be an amusing person but not that amusing to the point of being a clown. Women always choose those men who have a shared sense of humor. The more she smiles, the more she opens to you. For this reason, making your wanted girl smile is essential. There is another benefit of making her smile. When the girl is alone, she may remember you and smile once again. Thus, you may enter her heart. To flirt with a girl, you should get into her heart. You can make some jokes also to make her smile.

Tell Her She is Beautiful

Women are always conscious of their appearance, body, and costumes. Matching them is a good and straightforward way to flirt with them. Whenever you see your preferred girl using a stunning dress, never waste time to tell her that she is looking gorgeous in the dress. Tell her that this dress suits her a lot. It will have a great impact on her. If she uses that dress in another t, your complimentary remark will be remembered, and you will be in her idea. By doing this, you can move another step towards her. Keep getting closer to her and wait for the day you are valuing.

To flirt with your wanted girl, you should always watch her to catch any sort of changes in her look or appearance. For instance, the girl you like may have a new hairstyle. As you see her, you should talk about it. You can also add something like, "You are looking more stunning in this new hairstyle." It will send her a message indicating that you continuously observe her very carefully, and you are quite interested in her. Women like to be followed by men. She will understand that you are not one of those who only know how to say, "You are gorgeous" to impress girls.

Take Her Out

You can take her to someplace for lunch or dinner. Since there will be no nuisance between you and her, it can offer you more time and space. The girl will be pleased. She will also come to understand that you left the friendship zone. You can invite her to enjoy a movie picture with you in the theatre. At the cinema, you both will find a different environment. Make sure that the movie is romantic. If she comes with you to watch a romantic comedy, romantic scenes will move her a lot. She may consider you as her hero and find herself the heroine of that movie.

Appreciate Her Choice

If your preferred woman purchases something new, you must appreciate it. To flirt with her, you can not just stop here. You may tell her that her choice is exceptional and authentic. Tell her that her decision is a proof of her being an exception from other women. Every woman enjoys to present herself as different from other girls. Tell her to help you in choosing things if you want to buy something for yourself. As women like shopping, she may concur with your proposition. You need to buy what she accepts for you. If you do so, it may make her believe that you genuinely like her choices, and you value them. When you both are at the market to buy, if she selects something for her and does not purchase it for an unknown reason, you better purchase it secretly and give it to her the next day. It will shock her most, and women like to be surprised in this way. She will think that you genuinely care for her.

Inform her that you are eager to check her out

If your desired girl comes wearing a really attractive dress, you need to observe her from feet to head. Just keep looking at her. You need to tell her that she is looking hot when she is about to leave. It will make her feel attractive. Women just love this feeling. The more you can provide her with this kind of opportunity of feeling hot, the more you pave the way for dating her.

Using Text

A man can quickly use his phone or social media to flirt with ladies. Try to build up a relationship of exchanging texts with your wanted girl. The language of your text must cross the line. In your texts, call her using the sweet words and try to use her nickname. Whenever you find her phone switched off or she is offline, simply send messages like "Anything wrong?", "Are you OK?" "Miss you." When she is going to open her cellular phone or will be online, she will find your texts and may think about you positively. She will text you back, and therefore interaction will take place so well between you and her. It will help you a lot to flirt with her and win her heart.

You can compare "Flirting a Girl" to a game. In the game, you use some tricks and tips to win, here to win in flirting with women you also need the same procedure and techniques.

Get noticed

You can not get the chance to flirt with a girl unless you get noticed. Your personality, look, smartness will come to no use, if you stop working on getting seen by women. So, getting noticed is nonetheless really essential. Just wearing beautiful clothing and having a cool hairstyle will not help you to get observed unless you use your eyes as a medium of communication and make facial expressions very well. This chapter will tell you about how you can make a woman notice you.

Eye Contact

To flirt with a girl, you need to make eye contact with her through her eyes, and it is essential for your purpose. A correct usage of eye contact can provide you with your required steps for this mission. She will notice you among thousands of people if you can manage an accurate eye contact with a girl. Try to keep your eyes directly to her eyes. Do not take a look at something else until she takes a look at you and finds that you are staring at her. The girl will try to find out what you have to say through your eyes. The more she tries, the more you enter into her head. This is a fantastic benefit for anyone. As it will make her consider you all the time and gradually she might get a special feeling for you. In this situation, your opportunities for dating this girl increases at a high rate.

Staring

We can quickly discover whether a woman and a man sitting in front of us are a couple or not. The lovers use to look at each other in various ways. They do not practice glance; instead, they keep looking at each other for an extended period. While flirting with a girl, keep gazing at her. A prolonged staring will have a terrific influence on her.

When a man gets his desired girl with no one around her, he usually feels like kissing her. If he does so, without any progress in flirting with her, she may get upset. Thus his date can get completed in no time. So, in the beginning, he needs to make her notice about what he is asking for. If you are wise enough, you can do that quickly. In the beginning, look at her lips and eyes. She will be able to know what you are saying if she gets interested in you. As she completes her speech, you just appreciate her speech and kiss her. Now she will not get upset anymore.

Facial expression

You can use your facial expression to get noticed. Whenever you are in front of a lady, keep a lovely expression on your face. Whenever she talks with you, keep your face directly at her. Some individuals have a bad practice of keeping their hands on their faces or looking here and there while talking. You better prevent it. You can bite your lips with your teeth, if you want to make you look a bit serious. You likewise can bring a gentle smile on your face. You need to look at her a couple of times if your preferred girl stands right behind you. However, do not make any obscene expression. Just try to tell her through your declaration that you have started liking her.

How to Get Her Begging to You ASAP

It is important to learn the interesting flirting games that have women passing away to see you once again. Due to the fact that you challenge her in a lively manner, these games can help build connections and make her comfortable.

Challenging a woman is the very best way to create a sexual urge. It tickles the playful side of women. Don't forget that no matter how you challenge her, you need to involve some type of touching.

When dealing with a woman who delights in a lively challenge, simply be sure that the games you play are enjoyable, and you use them.

In specific circumstances, you can get her to really compete with you. This is a great way to build sexual tension. But if you are bad with initiating that level of physical contact, you can begin it with another challenge like who can send out a text much faster.

Just keep in mind that the most crucial guideline for flirting is that you increase the attraction and capture her attention with secret and interest.

CONCLUSION

Here is a fast wrap-up of all the main flirting strategies, techniques, and tips talked about in this book.

Flirting is subtle. You need to indicate attraction, rather than straight-out state it playfully. Create secret, be vague, indicate instead of the state, and, most importantly, be lively.

It is very vital to understand the distinction between friendly small talk and sexual flirting. Flirting is not the same as the fun, friendly small talk you have with your male buddies. Flirting is far more sexual-- not straight sexual (as stated above), but indirect. If you banter with her in a friendly way, you'll most likely than not end up in the friend zone. So ensure you playfully weave in sexual undertones.

When women 'shit test' you, such as by making a rude remark, asking an unpleasant question, or poking and prodding for possible insecurities of yours, just amplify and concur whatever she says.

Act like you're the reward. This is a gratifying and playful method of flirting. Simply reframe the conversation-- or any of her actions as if she is the one chasing after (and trying to seduce) you.

Have a strong frame of mind. This is probably among the essential elements of flirting, because your frame of mind comes everything else.

When you find yourself needing a fast refresher on the fundamentals of flirting, you may review all the strategies in this book and get on your way.

Now. all you have to do is put this book down and start! Best of luck!

DATING ESSENTIAL FOR MEN

Alpha Male Strategies, Social Skills To Create A Relationship, Online Dating Tips And Effortlessly Attract More Women

INTRODUCTION

First of all, thank you for making an effort to get this book. This book is a concentration of everything I've found out and used to become successful. Not just that, but the information shared in the book is a selection of practical things that have been used to train other men to become very productive with dating.

As you embark on your journey towards self-improvement as a man, assume that the knowledge you gain from this book works till tested otherwise.

This book lays it on the line for you regarding what women find appealing in a man and shows you step-by-step how you can not just act in appealing ways only but also become an attractive man. And when you become a handsome man, you'll attain your dreams just by being yourself.

A personal note to those of you who may be thinking: "Yeah, sounds great, but I am who I am, and that isn't changing." Bullshit. Change is in your mind. As you picture, so you will be. Ninety percent of being successful thinks you can be successful. We're talking about the psychological picture here, which is a strategy that nearly all leading athletes use. They envision themselves achieving success.

Think of this for a moment: let's pretend you just won the lottery game, won big. You've got a million dollars. If you were to stroll into a club tonight, do you believe you'd walk more confidently? Project yourself with more authority? Sure, you would! Girls often understand when a man's got something, be it money, power, or anything, just by the way he manages himself.

And I'm going to show you not just how to manage yourself, but how to truly be more confident, so that your walk and talk almost yell to the world, "Hey, I am confident!".

Women have somehow evolved to be instinctively and intensely drawn to strong and dominant alpha males-- not wussy, weak "nice guys.".

Unfortunately, very few men are born natural alpha males. Most of the alpha males out there are self-made, learning to develop within themselves the fundamental traits that make alpha males the amazing, effective, positively intimidating men that they are.

The primary aim of this book is to equip you with the tools you require and the qualities you need to develop in order to become an alpha male having fantastic success with the dating game. Dive right in, get started, and find the crucial traits you need to become an alpha male.

CHAPTER ONE

First Date

Where do I take her to on the first date, and what can I do to make a great impression?

That very first date is special and is something that many women will ruminate upon and ponder as lots of women take much enjoyment from this time of being wooed and getting romantic attention. This is the reason why men might feel under pressure to get it. Trying to get it right can be a battle for some low self-esteem guys, especially attempting to consider somewhere unique to take her or what to plan. Many will suggest a sumptuous meal, which can work quite well as it provides a focus. Food can give a subject of conversation, specifically if the woman takes pleasure in cooking, eating, or baking out. Going out for a meal does involve lengthy conversations, and some low self-esteem guys may have a hard time with this and may prefer just to meet for a fast drink or coffee.

If continuing a chat is difficult or concern, then an excellent option may be to go to the movie theatre or to listen to a band or orchestra as this will limit the communication and offer a common interest to discuss in the interval or when the program has finished.

If, though, the couple have met through a dating website and have not seen each other before, it may be much better to keep the meeting quick, if this is the case perhaps meeting for a couple of drinks or a coffee would be safer and permit the chance to make a rash retreat.

Having a shared interest works well in relationships and is a fantastic way for couples to meet. I have worked with some men who discover some voice tones or accents, particularly irritating. If this were the case, then it would be meaningless to pursue a relationship with the individual. Having said this, for some guys talking on the telephone is not always a simple option, and I have worked with some men who have a real worry of using the phone and find it hard to sound confident and articulate.

If a male turns up on a date looking neglected, with foul breath or body smell, it is not likely he will see her for a 2nd date if this is the very best he can do to impress her. Providing time and factors to consider to looks and health is essential. It is also a great idea not to consume anything ahead of time that is going to duplicate and result in the lady being showered with offending burps. Halitosis is a significant turn off for a lot of individuals, and women do appear to revel in good smells, so if a male uses aftershave or deodorant, it can go a long way.

Whatever the couple decides to do on the first date, the man must remember that many women do delight in a little love. It can be the basic things the man does that will offer the female a long-lasting and great impression of their date and will go far in making her feel both feminine and special. The guy could make an effort to open the door for the lady, bring her some flowers, compliment her appearance; he might be the one to go to the bar for beverages or merely stroll on the outside of the pavement. At the end of the night, he could provide to walk her to her car, bus stop, or house. If she is on her way home, try sending a text to guarantee she got home securely. This will all be noted and remembered by her. These little gestures can make so much distinction to how the female will feel, both about herself and her date.

The Worst First Date Mistakes Guys Make

When you are setting up to go out with someone, you need to prevent making mistakes. With the website modern age, you are going to have the ability to see what the worst first date mistakes people make are, and how to avoid them. Although you could search online for the worst first date mistakes people make, you will find that numerous women will affirm the reality that men still make errors. There are a couple of things that you can do to ensure that you're not anywhere near the issue areas if you desire to prevent making any errors. With that in mind, the following tips will use in almost any circumstance.

- Program Up Late

The very first thing that you need to advise yourself about is straightforward, be on time. In truth, don't merely be on time, be early. Amidst the worst very first date errors people make, time is everything. Don't' be late, and search the location before the date. In fact, go to the place where you're going to meet your date and walk, look at some signals, and see what to anticipate. You are going to be able to eliminate a bit of the nerve that usually comes with first dates if you do this.

- Focus on her only

You shouldn't be browsing in front of her. Check out her eyes, and let her be your world. Do not under any situations take a look around for other women, even if there are gorgeous girls all around. You have to stay focused. You need to flirt with her, speak with her, listen, and take notice of the words that are coming out of her mouth. Do not attempt to alter subjects, try to stay within her viewpoint, and do whatever it takes to avoid the worst first date errors people make. If you can't do this, then you're not ready to date on a major level.

- Make Her Pay

The biggest problem that a lot of women have on very first dates is that their partner does not pay for things. You ought to be all set to pay for things. Rather, you must pay for her supper, coffee, or easy aspects. Making her pay is the wrong concept. Instead, focus on spending for the date.

Do not spend the very first date discussing your special interests.
What should I talk about on the very first date?

What to talk about on the very first date is typically a significant concern for many men. Small talk and Asperger syndrome do not go well together, and for someone with

AS initiating and maintaining irrelevant social chit chat is nearly impossible. It requires a lot of ideas and effort on their part.

The majority of women will desire to feel that the guy has an interest in them and is pleased with her appearance. They will anticipate him to be able to make them feel good, and an excellent way to start is by using a compliment about how she looks. The guy may compliment her hair, her smile, her fragrance, or what she is wearing. To have a couple of rehearsed compliments can be helpful and certainly assist break the ice when you first meet. Be careful about making comments that are too personal or sexual at this early phase in dating as this could be translated as sexual thoughts, which for some will feel too forward or threatening. Remarking that she has generous boobs or a voluptuous bottom is not likely to be well gotten at this stage.

There is a general rule of topics to prevent at this early stage in the courtship unless it is currently understood that both individuals share the same opinion as each other. These are:

- Politics
- Religion
- Morality
- Sex
- How to discipline children
- Women chauffeurs
- Her look, weight, or gown sense (unless complimentary).
- Third World.
- Capital penalty.

- Mental health.
- Physical health.
- His unique interest (unless it is shared or she expresses an interest in it).
- If his ex

At the end of the evening, it is always rewarding to attempt to complete on a welcome note, which can quickly be attained by him stating how much he has taken pleasure in the night, the conversation, and the business. If the man has chosen, he wants to see the woman again, then he can state so. It is best not to anticipate that the female will desire to organize it with him there and then. It is merely a way of letting her know he is delighted to see her once again. However, he wants to let her call him when she is free. By doing this, she will not feel under pressure and will value him offering her time to think about. She may well want to arrange another date there and then, which will feel great; however, if she does not do this and neither does she make contact, then the man needs to leave it there and not pester her with texts and calls.

How do I know when or if to take it further?

In my research, I asked females to explain what attracted them to their partners, and the details that came back generally shared the very same thread throughout. Lots specified that they felt the guy they are contented with is a complete gentleman; they explained him as gentle, kind, peaceful, well mannered, attentive, and having other favorable qualities, all of which they recognized early on in their very first meeting. The women were very taken by the men that valued them and did not put pressure on them to be physically intimate.

So how can a guy learn what she desires? One method to inspect out if she wants more than a platonic relationship with him is for him to touch her in a way that is friendly and not sexual and see how she reacts. For instance, if they have gone out for a meal and her hands are on the table, he may attempt resting his hand by hers and see if she moves her hand closer or if she rapidly pulls her hand away. Then the male may gently take her hand and hold it in his if she does not pull away. When they are walking together, the guy might use his arm to link or ask if he may hold her hand. Asking authorization is always the safest method, but for some men, their worry of rejection is so intense that they discover they can not ask the question. What if the woman says no? If this is the case, it might feel much safer to use texting or emailing to ask if she would like more from the relationship or not.

Texting or emailing has been a lifesaver for some men, and using this form of communication has felt much safer for them. An ideal time to text is typically after a date, saying something like:

' Hello Mary. You looked absolutely beautiful tonight; it was challenging for me not to kiss you! Love John x'.

Once this is sent, he will need to wait to see what she sends outback. The female might text, stating she is not prepared for that or does not feel that way. If she does, then it is significant that he had discovered before he did try to take it even more and found himself in an uneasy and challenging scenario. Or she just might say:' Thank you, John. Yes, I wish you had kissed me! '.

How can I know when or if to take it even more?

If it is the latter, then he has his response, and next time the couple meets up, he may wish to try a mild kiss at the end of the date.

You may have discovered I USED the wording 'gentle kiss' how a person kisses are essential for most women and also often seen as indicating what type of enthusiast the guy will be. The very first kiss is something that the lady will remember and replay in her mind. This is an essential relocation, and it is another part of dating that the guy requires to attempt to get right; it can practically be seen as the crossroads that will take the dating into an intimate relationship or end it dead in its tracks.

Kissing should be respectful and romantic; it must be soft, gentle, and focused. For some women, there is absolutely nothing worse than being kissed in a manner that might leave them feeling as though their mouths have been powerfully raped! There is absolutely nothing worse than being kissed by someone who is intrusive with their tongue or covers the woman's mouth with their saliva. These are significant turn-offs and will signal to the female that if this is how the male kisses, then this is how he will treat her in bed.

Another rule is for the man not to translate a kiss as a free license to begin touching the lady's breasts, bottom, or vagina. The man may stroke the non-erogenous places of her body such as her back, arms or her hair but that should be as far as he takes it at this phase unless she makes it extremely obvious by offering a clear physical or spoken sign that she would like more from him, for example, if she touches the guy's penis or verbally asks him to touch her. Even then, it would still be worth him checking it out by asking her the question.

After the kiss, it would make her feel great if he complimented her, such as informing her he has wanted to kiss her, considering that he first met her or that she is gorgeous. It is the small things he does that she will keep in mind at this phase. For him to show her regard while letting her understand, he finds her a very desirable female will all belong to the journey into the next phase, the sexual stage.

When again the signs a woman gives off that she is drawn into a male can be very subtle and not easy to read; the factor for this is that the woman does not want to get it incorrect either. Many women still hold on to the notion that it is for the man to initiate or to make the first repositioning and will frequently likewise hold the belief that he will have read her non-verbal signals that it is OK to make a relocation, such as hold her hand or kiss her.

CHAPTER TWO

Dating Rules for Men

The best place to meet a prospective partner?

The task of finding a prospective partner can seem overwhelming for the guy with low self-esteem. To cover every possible avenue would be difficult as relationships can grow out of the most unlikely situations and encounters. I have selected the most likely locations and the most accessible. Everybody will have a choice, and what will match one person might not suit another-- it will be for the reader to choose what might work best for them. Four of the most common locations are highlighted alongside their advantages and disadvantages

The night club

This way of meeting girls is rarely effective for some men. The majority will find night clubs traumatic due to the possibility of sensory overload, triggered by the loud music, flashing lights, crowded bars, and dance floors, which all tend to form a big portion of the night club scene. When faced with the distraction of so much background sound, sensory overload can feel extremely overwhelming, and some men have actually reported finding it difficult to hold a discussion. If the guy wants to interact with a woman he is trying to develop a connection with, this can feel quite difficult.

However, on the other hand, some men may find such location as a bonus as they can use the loud noise as a reason to avoid little talk and long discussions. This eases the pressure of having to consider what to say, and they can simply enjoy the dancing.

For the majority of men, however, there is a propensity to avoid night clubs, and this could be due to a history of disappointments. There have been accounts of men being set up by women to make their partners jealous, or just being used to buy drinks. It is recommended that if the club is a choice being considered, you should go there with a group or with a good friend who can be depended on for suggestions or to spot the caution signs. Sadly this is not often possible for some men, and they can end up feeling both overwhelmed and confused by the whole experience.

If a woman approaches a man in a club, he has to ask himself: Why? He needs to assure himself she is not with another man and merely trying to make that man generous. If unsure, he should ask her if she is with her partner. If she asks for a drink in the very first few sentences, it would be reasonable to be cautious as it is likely she is using him just to get complimentary drinks. Nevertheless, asking her if she would like a drink, giving her a compliment, or dancing within her proximity can be ways of first approaching a lady in a club. If the lady declines the drink, overlooks the compliment, or goes far from his space on the dance floor, this implies she is not interested, and he should not pursue it.

If he is still with the woman at the end of the night, then he could suggest he wants to see her once again or ask if she would like to exchange mobile numbers to correspond. Then he must wish her well and make his way home if she says she would rather leave it for now. But if she says it would be good to see him once again or concurs to him giving her a lift home, he needs not to assume this means she desires sex. Unless she makes it very clear by saying so and asking if he wishes to have sex with her, the man must never assume that sex is on the program. Often bear in mind that as alcohol can promote an incorrect complacency, it can also trigger an absence of control. The man needs not to put himself at risk or become a danger to anyone else.

Pros:

- It is most likely to provide the opportunity of a one night stand if that is what you are trying to find.
- If you like dancing), - You get to dance
- It is much easier to lose yourself in the crowd.
- You will not be expected to talk much.
- There will be the opportunity to meet women of different backgrounds, cultures, and ages.

Cons:

- It is not perfect for finding a significant or long-lasting partner.
- It can cause sensory overload.
- Too much alcohol can trigger a wrong complacency and loss of control.
- There is a risk of someone reacting violently.

- There is a risk of being used to purchase drugs, drinks, or cigarettes.
- It can be restricted to a younger age.

Workplace

A large proportion of couples meet within a work environment. It does, nevertheless, need knowledge of what the company rules are, as some workplaces do not endure relationships within the workforce. To disregard this might result in one or both of the couples needing to leave their place of employment, and for many people, this would be both stressful and troublesome. The repercussion of this is most likely to have a negative effect on the relationship that has been recently developed.

Assuming the company does not prohibit relationships between personnel, the office can be a way of meeting a potential partner. Obviously, the kind of work a person does will make a difference to this, as some jobs can be male-controlled, such as engineering or IT. If, on the other hand, the work environment provides a combined climate and there is a lady that the man is attracted to, then the workplace can offer a perfect opportunity to learn more about somebody. It will provide both the opportunity to get to know each other gradually and to develop a connection before embarking on the possibility of a relationship. This all sounds extremely straightforward; the concern is that some men can not inform whether a lady is, in fact, attracted to them, or if she is merely enjoying their relationship and wants no more.

Starting a work-related relationship is, in some cases, left to gatherings such as the Christmas party, as this can achieve two things: (1) the guy can see if she features a partner, which would dismiss the possibility of taking it further, and (2) if she is alone, he can see if she looks out his company. If the Christmas party is not an alternative and as long as she is not using a wedding or engagement ring, then the man will need to do a little investigation to discover whether she is readily available. This could be achieved by asking someone who knows her if she has a partner and even asking her directly.

This needs tact, and the male should tread carefully so as to avoid intruding upon her level of sensitivities or to make himself susceptible to being rejected. One way forward might be to learn if any new restaurant has opened in the vicinity and then mention this and ask her whether she has been there or heard any reports about it. If she has a partner, this will give her the chance to let the man know, by saying that she went there with her boyfriend or is planning to choose him. Most women will be honest and make a potential pursuer to see if they are with someone, although this might not always be the case. If the man is on Facebook, he could ask her if she has a Facebook account, and if so, he might request to add her as a friend on Facebook-- this is likely to inform him of her relationship status.

If a man has found a lady in his work environment who he is attracted to, he will need to be cautious about how he approaches the possibility of a date with her. If she informs him she is with somebody or overlooks his efforts to strike up a conversation; then he should withdraw. If not, he might find himself the target of ridicule or, even worse, being reported for harassment.

Having stated that, work-based relationships are often effective, and couples have met this way. If the relationship is unsuccessful, the work environment can end up being a source of tension or distress, making it challenging for one or both to continue working there. If the man finds himself the target of destructive gossip, this can be made worse. All he can do is to put on a brave face, disregard the chatter and understand that these things quickly blow over, so long as he does not react.

Pros

- There might be a typical denominator between you.

- There might be time to construct up a relationship.

- If she is in a relationship already, - There might be the ability to check out.

- Work social events are a good time to meet someone.

- Relationships formed by doing this are typically successful.

Cons:

- Relationships might be restricted as part of the business's policy.

- It can be tough to determine if the female has a partner.

- It can be difficult to be sure whether her interest is romantic or simply platonic.

The job of discovering a potential partner can appear frustrating for the male with AS, and I am typically asked the best way to achieve this. If a female approaches a man in a club, he requires to ask himself: Why? He needs to assure himself she is not with another guy and merely attempting to make that man envious. Unless she makes it extremely clear by stating so and asking if he desires to have sex with her, the male needs never ever to presume that sex is on the program. If the man is on Facebook, he could likewise ask her if she has a Facebook account and if so, he might request to include her on his friend list.

The man could end up being talkative if he gets it wrong or reveals excessive information. But if the relationship ends, then it can make the work environment stressful.

Social Or Unique Interest Groups

A search on the internet might indicate that there is a social group for single grownups running in the local vicinity. Social groups are run by a particular set of individuals who interact, putting together a program of activities to hook up with new friends via the social platform. Members of the group then choose which occasions they would like to go to or take part in.

The cost of signing up with these groups can vary, and this will require to be inspected thoroughly. In addition, the age variety of the group will also need to be examined, as some groups can be for younger grownups in their twenties and thirties, whereas others will be for older age.

Social groups can be a terrific way to be familiar with others without the pressures of needing to try to form a relationship. Many will not be in a relationship and will just be searching for business and friends that they can hang out with, so be sure of the type of social group you are joining.

Numerous platforms offer a wide variety of activities and interests to select from, such as strolling, dancing, dining, theatre, and weekends away. They give the member the choice to engage as much as they like and to reoccur as they please.

As social groups, there are also interest groups such as the Ramblers (www.ramblers.org.uk), hill-walking groups, photography groups, and numerous others. These interest-specific groups can be perfect for a man if he has a particular interest, as he will have the ability to share this with others along with the social side of the group. A considerable benefit of meeting somebody in an interest group is that they will be someone who shares the same interest, and this will give both an excellent beginning point in developing a relationship.

Pros

- It will indicate there is someone to satisfy you.
- There is no pressure to have a relationship.
- You will have the ability to get to understand someone initially.
- There are lots of various venues and activities.

- You can discover somebody who shares your interests.

Cons

- You may not proceed with everybody in the group.
- Some groups are costly to charge or sign up with to join in the activities.
- Being part of a group might be effort and quite strenuous for you.

Dating Websites

Internet dating for numerous guys might appear to be an ideal choice as it offers the chance to select a woman beforehand they discover attractive from her photo and who seems to share their interests.

Being able to organize the first meeting is another significant bonus in using dating sites, and I have understood some guys go to excellent lengths to attempt to get this right. Let me share a story of a man that fixes a dinner where he had set up to meet his date the following night. He discovered a good place to park his automobile and inspected what change he may require for the parking meter, and he timed the length of time it took him to arrive by car and after that by foot to the dining establishment.

He selected a location for them to sit in and picked which seating position he preferred for himself, which in this case was to have his back against the wall. He studied the menu, chose what he would eat and how much it would cost, took down where is the toilet, and were about the white wines. By doing this, he reduced the worry part he suffered from unforeseeable issues on the night. When he went on to have his date, he was more relaxed and felt more positive than he would have. I am delighted to state that they went on to a 2nd date.

Website dating can allow the man to feel more in control than he would in a random situation; however, it mustn't become a way of life and a habit. Internet dating for some guys can become a fascination, which can be the failure of a relationship that could have worked. In some men, their capability to read other individuals' motives and covert agendas are complicated. This will often make them unable to tell whether someone is sly or friendly. This challenge in checking out others' intentions can make them vulnerable to exploitation when dating, especially to financial exploitation. This can make him a prime target for being taken off the expenses. If a guy discovers himself continually spending in a relationship, then he requires to draw back from being overgenerous and see what reaction this causes from the lady. If a female is authentic, then she will understand, compromise and arrangement will be made.

I have also encountered clients who have talked of women on dating websites from foreign countries who were very keen on marital relationships. It has later transpired that the women's primary intention for the relationship was to get to a brand-new house or car. Obviously, there is no other way he can be sure if her motives are real till they are together as a couple, but it might assist if he visits her in her place or if he introduces her to his family and friends to seek their opinion.

Nevertheless, after a while, when the relationship becomes more down to earth, and the enthusiasm subsides, he might feel dissatisfied and, after that, decide that she is wrong for him, that she deceived him. He might then decide that he has still not found the right female and begin the search all over again. I have understood this pattern to continue for several years for some guys until, eventually, they meet the right one.

Pros

- There is the opportunity to select someone who appears ideal.
- There is access to women from other cultures or nations.
- There is a chance to build a relationship using e-mail instead of needing to make a conversation.
- It is possible to have constructed a relationship with the first conference.
- A place and time for the meeting can be chosen.
- It enables the choice of inspecting the location ahead of time.

Cons

- You might not always get replies to your emails.
- Emails might not lead to a date.
- A date may not turn up.
- The person you meet may not look the very same as their photo.
- You might be set up for monetary gain or other benefits.
- If there is any chemistry between you. Until you meet the person, you will not understand.
- Internet dating can become a fixation.

How do I understand if she is drawn into me?

Never assume that her sensations are the very same as yours, and the tourist attraction is mutual.

If it is the first encounter and a woman is drawn into a man, she will look into his eyes, and she will likewise smile just a fleeting smile, and after that, she will look away. As long as he smiles back, she will watch again and smile. If they are already in communication, the man may discover that she leans her body towards him and maybe makes physical contact with him in conversation. For instance, she might affectionately touch his arm while talking. What do these natural gestures signal for a man?

The world of dating and all the complexities it brings can seem like a headache for guys, as it includes having the ability to read the other person's body language, facial expressions, and voice articulation. These are all things men will find extremely difficult to do. A female may be quite mindful of avoiding appearing over-keen in the early stages of the meeting as she may fear rejection.

Trouble in reading the social hints provided by others will cause an issue for man in getting the timing right in the dating game, as it will not come naturally for him. This can be made harder by the possibility that there might currently be a history of him being rejected by his peers and found out understanding that he can sometimes misread other individuals. This alone could significantly weaken his self-confidence in understanding whether he is getting the pacing.

The man will now remain in the scenario that he has discovered a lady he likes brought, but he is now left with no idea of whether his sensations and desires are reciprocated; moreover, if they are on a romantic or relationship level. If the female has vocalized her feelings, then this will not be a problem, but this is highly unlikely, as she may likewise fear rejection or the danger of being implicated of being too forward.

Determining whether the attraction is reciprocated can put some men through absolute torment, sometimes affecting both their health and frame of mind

Often problems can develop from the guy making the presumption that if he likes a lady, then she must feel the same about him, and the tourist attraction is shared. This is often not the case, and it is necessary that this is never ever presumed unless the female has definitely spelled out her sensations of destination to him. The reason this misassumption can occur is a lack of theory of the mind and not having the ability to see the circumstance from the other individual's viewpoint. The only frame of mind the man will be conscious of will be his sensations, and these feelings of attraction might be powerful. The strength of his impressions might be exaggerated due to his passion for finding a girlfriend, and it is this that may trigger him to presume that the lady shares his destination and feels as highly as he does.

This misreading can likewise happen in reverse, and I discover some clients can hold the belief that others are thinking adversely about them, simply by seeing another person's look or a look. They will miss the fact that a female is flirting with them or finds them appealing. The presumption might be wrong, and this is why it is essential to check out just what the lady feels before any action is taken. It is very important not to get too carried away by feelings of attraction to a specific female or to assume she feels the very same, as you may be too forward. The lady may feel men as being egotistical or arrogant, and his chances of charming her will be lost.

When a female is giving signals that she is drawn into a guy, she will keep eye contact a couple of seconds longer than would usually take place. Eye contact can be robust for some men to make, and they will have a problem with making or maintaining eye contact, particularly when in communication.

One of the reasons for this is that they might discover it tough to focus on what they or the other is saying if they are attempting to keep eye contact or read another individual's eye contact. I have actually discovered some will go to fantastic lengths to attempt to enhance this skill by going to neuro-linguistic shows (NLP) courses, checking out body language books, or just from observation of soaps and films.

I have noted some of the signs to look for that might show that a female is interested, or not, as the case may be.

Eye Contact

Interested

- She takes longer than usual eye contact.
- She averts and looks back rather rapidly.

Not interested

- She may avert.

- She might look down but offer brief darting glances.

Mouth

Interested

- She smiles; this can be minor.
- She sulks.

Not interested

- She does not smile at all.
- She will just smile at you in a welcoming or if you say something amusing.
- She will provide an extremely tight-lipped smile, which may suggest she is annoyed or worried.

Distance

Interested

- If sitting by you or in front of you, she will lean towards you.
- She will enable you to come into her area, or she will enter yours and stand or sit, preferably near you.
- Her arms will be open and welcoming.

Not interested

- She will lean away from you.
- She will ensure that there is no physical touch between you.
- She will keep her arms folded.

Touch

Interested

- She may make physical contact with you; this might be a pat, rubbing your arm, permitting her foot or knee to make contact with you.
- She might give a hug when bidding farewell or greeting you.

Not interested

- She will pull away from any physical contact.
- Her greetings and farewells will be quick and short, with no effort to touch you.

Body Movements

Interested

- She might keep having fun with her hair or pressing it back.
- Her arms are open.
- Her feet are pointed towards you.
- She maintains eye contact.

Not interested

- Her arms are folded.
- She averts.
- She looks past you.
- She points her feet far from you.

Interaction

Interested

- She asks concerns.
- She gives compliments.
- She chuckles with you (not at you).

Not interested

- She offers short one-syllable responses.
- She sighs.
- She does not ask you questions.

This list is not sure-fire, as it can not take into account a female's character; she may be shy and therefore feel nervous and show a closed body movement. On the other hand, some women are demonstrative and extremely tactile, and although they will appear friendly, they will not be flirting at all. It should likewise be taken into consideration whether a female has been drinking alcohol, as this will decrease her inhibitions, making her more likely to show flirty or affectionate behavior indiscriminately, if the man can ask someone else's viewpoint this would be useful. If this is not possible, then he may consider informing her in a text that he likes her and will quickly find by her reply if his feelings are reciprocated. He should appreciate this and not try to take it any further if the female feels the same, then that will be fantastic; if she does not.

She is unlikely to be offended by understanding he likes her. However, if he pursues her and does not respect her feelings, she will be offended, and he will get harass.

CHAPTER THREE

Dating Mistakes Made by Men and How to Avoid it

At the ripe aging of 23, a friend of mine got his very first girlfriend. Even though he was simply a law student, barely getting by, he continued to invest over thousands of dollars on the girl is simply one brief, whirlwind of a month, blowing through expensive wines at restaurants and other unnecessary presents. My pal was sad for months later, not to point out that he had to get a part-time task to renew his bank account.

Been there, done that. I've bought girls suppers, motion pictures even a $500 ring that I saved up for back in high school. It used to be that I 'd routinely bring a girl a $30 arrangement of flowers on our first date.

All I 'd desired out of the deal was to get laid. It appeared a fundamental deal the chick would get the stuff I purchased for her, and in exchange, all she needs to do is spread her legs.

Sound familiar? Are you annoyed when you don't get laid like you should, after all the cash you've invested?

Well, here are the essential things: you're running on a false assumption. Money invested doesn't always equal legs opening.

The problem with lavishing cash on a lady who hasn't accepted, communicate a negative message to her.

I understand that saying "do not buy things for ladies" Men are brought up to think that if there's something of worth that we desire, we require to be ready to shell out what it takes to buy it? Well, when it comes to inanimate items that don't believe on their own, that's real.

Here are some of the errors.

- Revealing off Your Cash

This is continuously a typical error most men make during dating. Usually, men like to reveal ladies they have the money even on the first date. This can be extremely hazardous. An accountable lady searching for the right guy may neglect your cash. To date effectively as a guy, you have to be very simple and charming. Keep the woman in the dark up until you come nearer to her.

- Being Arrogant

Numerous men appear to be strong-headed when they head out to date. Sure, men can be bossy because it is innate in them. There's always the need to mellow down when you desire to satisfy a woman. You have to indulge a lady and reveal her just how much you care as you date her. You can't attain this if you're too strong-headed and bossy.

- Excess Talking without listening

Some men talk too much when they go out for a date. For the most part, such men will continuously keep talking about their achievements in life. They find it tough to give their partners enough area to talk. When their partners are talking, they also discover it difficult to listen. This can be very dangerous. A dating relationship is a two-way thing. You have to offer the other individual sufficient room to talk. When dating a girl, you require to give her modification to air her views. When she's talking, you likewise have to listen to her.

- Speaking about an ex while staying with the new date.

Many men make this mistake. They keep speaking about their unsightly experience with their ex sweethearts as they meet their new dates. This can be appalling. When you're dating a brand-new girl, there's no point going over about your ex. If you keep doing that, you can quickly put her off. You suppose to focus on how to keep the brand-new woman pleased as you consult with her on a regular basis.

- Demanding for sex prematurely

Many men likewise make this mistake! They quickly ask sex, even at the preliminary stages of the relationship. You need to avoid this if you truly wish to enjoy dating a girl. A cheap woman can quickly fall to your sex demand; however, this may be the beginning of problems in the relationship.

Avoid the habits below, and you'll instantly separate yourself above 95% of the other men out there. That by itself, when women notice it, right away makes them feel wetter around you.

1. Bragging

" You must see my amazing home."

" I'm about to get a raise approximately six figures a year!" "I have a huge cock."

High self-confidence is attractive to women. Think highly of yourself, and a female will think extremely of you.

It's alright to make an obvious joke about putting yourself down(said with a playful tone of voice)

Frequently, men do make typical dating mistakes. If you're a guy interested in dating, there's a need for you to understand more about the standard errors and how to avoid them.

2. Putting other individuals down

And because women are delicate creatures who sympathize with the less lucky. Don't put down people who are your sexual competitors, because that too reveals your insecurity. Instead just don't take note of them, since they're not worthwhile of your attention.

Never make a big offer out of it when you do purchase the female things. Say something like, "I'll pay for the coffee. It's no big deal." What that states to her is that you're more interested in the social interaction that the two of you are having, which you barely believe about the beverage you just bought her.

It also means that there are no strings attached. By stating, "it's no huge deal," you make it clear that you're not putting pressure on her to reciprocate what you've provided for her.

" Buying me things since he wants something later" is a behavior that numerous women think about manipulative and results in the male being denied sex. And to be rather honest, lots of men fall right into that trap by making a big production out of purchasing the woman nice things. Don't be that guy.

The main thing you require to do is to realize why you're doing something.

Never purchase things for a female or do favors for her because you believe you need to make her approval. Instead, adopt the frame of mind of the dominant male: anything you provide for her is conditional on her having earned it.

Tips For Success in Online Dating for Men.
Women do receive a lot of offers, but many of them fall under one of a selected variety of categories. If you are sending a girl an e-mail, and it falls under among the following classifications, she will most likely delete it and move on.

I understand that this may seem unreasonable - after all, you put in the time to compose to her, so definitely she owes you the common decency of composing back?

Again, incorrect.

If a lady is especially appealing, it's not uncommon for her to receive 50 or perhaps 100 brand-new e-mails every day. She simply does not have time to go through each one and reply. So she needs to produce psychologically faster ways that separate the wheat from the chaff. She will scroll down her list of e-mails, declining most without even opening them, just stopping to open the ones that stimulate her interest in some method.

Here are six typical mistakes that you can prevent that will set you ahead of the competitors.

1. Having no subject line, or a dull subject line in your initial e-mail to her.

Many people just put 'hi' in the subject line of the email. Believe about what happens when she logs on and sees 50 new emails; all showed in a list. All she can see is your username and the subject line of your email. If 49 of the e-mails say 'hi' as the subject line, and one e-mail has a different subject, which is probably to catch her attention? So think of how to make yourself stand apart from the crowd.

2. Sending out overtly sexual preliminary emails.

This ought to be a no brainer, but considering that numerous guys are doing it, it requires a reference. If you send her an overtly sexual first e-mail, she will think 'pervert,' delete you and probably block you at the same time. Yes, women indeed enjoy sex as much as men, including filthy talk; however, there is a location and a time.

What kind of reaction would you expect if you strolled up to her on the street and began spewing a lot of filth talk at her? You get the same response online - other than you simply don't get to see the action. You simply get deleted.

3. Sending an uninteresting first email.

A lot of very first e-mails from men fall under this classification. Example: 'Hey there, my name is John, and I read your profile and liked the appearance of you. I see you like cooking and tennis. I like cooking and tennis too, so I feel we have something in common. Inspect my profile and compose back if you like what you see.'.

I assure you - if she's been on the dating website for any length of time, she has read that same e-mail 100 times. It's the very same problem as number 1) on this list - you are not separating yourself from the crowd. You are not creating a spark of excitement in her brain that makes her wish to strike the reply button.

4. Not having an excellent set of images in your profile.

Typically she will read your very first email, and presuming you have created some kind of interest within her, she will open up your profile. What does she see recalling at her? A single, rough cam taken photo that appears like you're locked away in your bedroom someplace. Does that give the image of a social, fun guy who has lots of pals and is fun to be around? Nope. So you require to get out with friends in numerous social settings (not only bars) and get some great images taken that appear like you are having a good time. It will make all the difference in terms of the impression.

5. Having a profile filled with spelling mistakes or 'txt spk.'

Unless you're 12 years old, 'txt spk' is not cool. So compose in full sentences, at least provide the impression and attempt that you went to school. And there's no reason for being sloppy and having a profile loaded with spelling errors. In the back of her mind, she will be believing 'if he makes this little effort on his dating profile, how much effort does he took into the rest of his life?' Not a great start.

6. Having a boring profile.

Comparable to the boring very first e-mail, the uninteresting profile is the most common issue that most people have. Essentially their profile details a list of hobbies 'I like fishing, football, reading, tennis, climbing up, the movies, nights in and nights out. Email me if you like the same.' Absolutely nothing exciting there. You need to attempt and paint a photo with your words. Get her picturing the situation in her mind and explain it in brilliant detail. When she reads it, she will envision herself there with you, which is the initial step to her belonging to your life.

So it may take you half an hour to spruce up your profile. And you might require to take a few minutes to read her profile in future and think about an intriguing or amusing e-mail to send her that ignites her curiosity enough to think 'I want to learn more about this man' and hit the reply button.

Trust me that additional time will be well invested when you have your pick of stunning charms eager to snaffle you up and make you their man.

Error 1: Using bad pictures.

The Internet has ended up being a place full of fraudsters who develop dating profiles just to fulfill women and ask them for money if you have not already realized by now. These fraudsters generally only have one image in their profile; hence it is the norm for the majority of knowledgeable individuals who date online to believe that one picture profiles do not show the real individual. So start publishing several images of yourself, particularly ones where you are enjoying yourself together with your friends to reveal that you have a correct social life.

Error 2: Being impolite or nasty.

When she does not reply to your e-mail right away due to your frustration, in some cases, it is tempting to send a lady a nasty e-mail. However, you have got to keep your mood under check. Simply send one polite follow-up email if she doesn't respond and after that proceed. You have got to understand that attractive women get hit on a lot online, and they receive lots of e-mails daily.

Error 3: Not reading any profiles.

If you haven't realized it by now, most women dislike getting emails that are basic and do not discuss anything about their profile. Although it might take a while at the start because you need to go through their profiles and after that send a lot of emails with comments related to their profiles, it is worth it at the end.

Error 4: Being interested too quickly.

A lot of men are brought in by appearances, and frequently they simply discover a profile they choose and like that they like the female or are interested in the lady currently. This is probably a grave mistake to make as you don't know anything about her life at all, and for you, all understand she may have posted phony photos or pushed her profile. Instead, use online dating sites to meet lady offline to get to understand more about her.

Error 5: 'Dating' online.

Although there is no doubt that online dating websites are a terrific place to satisfy women, they are most likely one of the worst places to construct a relationship. You ought to attempt to get her phone number as soon as possible and arrange a meet-up offline as soon as you meet or discover somebody you are interested in. Don't waste your time dating online as you never know whether the person behind that profile is real or just out to bring you for a ride.

CHAPTER FOUR

Are you Mr.Nice Guy?

I'm going to try to describe precisely why a lady is not going to wish to end up with a Mr. Nice.

Unless she is totally out of alternatives, hopeless, and somewhat desperate. Then I think it's safe to say that she might not be that much of a quality lady after all, if this is the case. In any occasion, here are the reasons why good people are more turned down, discarded, and cheated on by the women who are in their ideal minds:

1. Nice Guys Have Difficulty Doing the RIGHT Thing.

Yeah, you heard me. Great guys have a great deal of trouble doing what is right in a specific scenario. Instead of doing what's right, good guys tend to decide for there a lot easier path and choose to do what is nice. If you can't do the best thing, then that suggests you make choices based upon trying to keep everybody else happy rather than making sure that you'll enjoy it yourself.

Since this will make you a pushover to her and anyone else, a female who has her actions together will not tolerate this. She'll see you as the type of man that is easily led by others and who is incapable of taking the required actions to makes things right in any given situation.

If you are a good person that does the great thing instead of the ideal thing, she'll merely see you as being unreliable. She'll realize that you won't have the ability to manage the disputes of life, which you will not have the ability to show individual stability.

2. Being Mr. Nice Guy Makes You Seem Less Authentic.

As a man, it's essential to be as authentic as possible in the choices that you make. It's just a part of being a fully grown guy. Great guys tend to have a problem with credibility because they will state "yes" to any request that comes their way.

Good people likewise have a difficult time sorting through the massive amounts of demands upon their time and resources.

In other words, nice people allow a lot of unnecessary commitments in their lives. Their lives are merely filled with excessive "fluff." They deal with other people's concerns, other individual needs, and other individuals' plans. Great people place themselves second to everything and everyone else, and that makes typically them a disposing ground for others.

You can be assured that no female is going to want a male who is a discarding ground for somebody else. If you can't be real to yourself, a female will simply feel as if you will not be true to her. She will not be able to feel secure with you, and thus her capability to become intimate with you will be incredibly limited, if at all possible.

3. Nice Guys Give Their Power Away to Women.

You've probably been allowing women (mom, sister, partner, girlfriend, etc.) to make the most critical choices of your life, and even the not-so essential ones as well. You've probably established a sort of relationship with women where you need to have them enjoy with you for you to be delighted with yourself. And think me; you don't wish to be in this type of situation.

Why? Well, if a female sense that you quickly offer your power away to her, she might recognize that you might do it for another woman. She'll question what makes her so unique anyhow.

What she wants is a guy in control of himself, and at times, her too. Providing your power away to a female just suggests that you offer her the approval to authorize you, which you've given her the enjoyment of ensuring that your requirements are always fulfilled.

This is a no-no.

No woman in her best mind wants a man to provide his power away to her. She will feel pushed into the position of being the "man in charge," and she will not like it. She dislikes it. And even worse, she hates men who make her feel that method.

Why Nice Guys Never Win With Women.

Remember, how no female in her right mind would wish to be with Mr. Nice-Guy? Well, fortunately for Mr. Nice-Guy, we have lots of women out there who are not entirely in their ideal minds at all. Because he can still put other people's requirements before his and keep a relationship with a lady, this is fantastic for our friend Mr. Nice-Guy. However, what sort of lady will he attract or perhaps create precisely?

Well, since of the way good people treat people, they tend to bring in numerous types of women that might prey upon their gullible, ignorant, and excessively kind-hearted ways. Even worse, they end up creating women like this as they end up being passive in their relationships. They might attract women with all sorts of problems, whatever from mentally clingy women to gold-diggers. You 'd be surprised at the kinds of women that good people naturally attract without even recognizing it.

There is an old cliché that says that there is somebody out there for everyone. I think its kind of real considering that a nice man and his manipulative methods can discover some measure of what he feels is joy in a relationship with a similarly manipulative female that truly desires to control the relationship or control. No man in his best mind would want to be in a relationship with a damaged and manipulative lady.

Don't get me wrong here; I understand that nobody is perfect and that everybody is going to have their problems in a relationship, however that does not suggest that you must go out trying to find the worst of the bunch since you do have the choice to avoid it.

A nice guy may attract a very possessive lady that will put high needs on his time and resources. Being the nice person that he is, he'll discover to bear with her high

179

demands to keep her pleased thinking that he's doing the right thing when in fact, he's merely doing the great thing. At the same time, he's suffering within, getting fed up, and internally contravened attempting to please this woman and trying to keep himself pleased and sane.

This guy is suffering because of his lack of individual borders. The more he neglects her habits and accepts it as something that he needs to deal with, the more he will suffer internally and begin to do not like the female and even worsen himself. No lady can appreciate him if he can not respect himself. The great man may soon find out that without self-regard, he can never discover true happiness in a relationship with his ideal woman.

In brief, a top-quality woman likes and wants a guy that has a high sense of pride. It is a necessity.

Man, who considers himself 'high-quality,' needs to be with a female who understands how to respect his limits. Anything less will be unfulfilling, unsatisfying, and entirely unsustainable to him.

10 Things You Should Know About the Nice Guy.

So before I reveal you how to tackle eliminating your Mr. Nice-Guy personality, let's see exactly just how much of these nice man beliefs and behaviors you are struggling with. Here are ten things you MUST understand about the Nice Guy:

1. A nice person believes that if he is excellent, offering, and caring, he will get joy, love, and satisfaction from others in return. He plays a sort of game with himself thinking that he deserves to be dealt with a particular method because of his niceness.

2. The nice guy offers to do things for a lady he barely knows. He has a strong desire to get the approval of women. This can be any female, specifically the ones that he discovers appealing and deserving of his excess amounts of niceness.

3. The nice guy avoids disputes by keeping his opinions or may even end up being reasonable with a woman when he does not actually concur. This nice person tends to think that in order to keep the peace and preserve the love and appreciation from a lady, he must concur with her at all expense. If it costs him his self-regard, he does this even.

4. The nice guy tries to take and fix the care of all her problems. He is drawn to attempting to help a lady out in any method that he possibly can. This is one of the primary reasons a nice person tends to bring in a lot of damaged women. His desire to

be her Mr. Fix-It makes him vulnerable to fall into relationships with problematic women.

5. The nice guy has an overwhelming need to seek approval from other people. It's the type of approval looking for, whereas he might feel guilty for stating "no" to somebody, or he may end up being uneasy with himself when he's disrespectful, even if it's out of necessity.

6. The nice person attempts to conceal his perceived flaws and mistakes from others. Due to the fact that he wants everyone's approval and he wishes to be seen in the finest light possible, he's ready to go to extreme lengths to make himself look as flawless as humanly possible. He's manipulative to the third degree.

7. The nice guy is always searching for the proper way to do things rather than simply making an effort at something. The nice guy is afraid of stopping working and, of course, making a mistake in front of others. He does not desire to step on anyone's toes. Because he does not want to rock the boat, he 'd rather not do anything if he does not have all the responses. Sadly, his fear of failure and criticism culminates in meaningless perfectionism and continuous procrastination. He not does anything and accomplishes less than nothing.

8. The nice guy tends to over-analyze everything instead of feeling things out for himself. In some cases, the nice person can be a bit of a perfectionist, and preferably of just going with the circulation and just letting things occur, he 'd rather have whatever planned and represented in his own best universe.

9. The nice guy has trouble making his needs a concern. Instead, he 'd rather pretend that what he wants.

Isn't that important and that he's a team gamer. Or he'll believe that by putting his requirements on the back burner he's one hell of a man which everybody ought to always bear in mind that he's such an excellent man which everybody needs to like him.

10. The nice guy is quite often mentally dependent on his woman. He's so reliant on his lady for his psychological wellness that he'll go through terrific lengths to guarantee that his woman's needs are satisfied before his and that he always gets her approval. Since in the end, he thinks that as long as she's delighted, he's happy.

Why You Must Kill the Nice Guy Inside.

When life presses you around, do you press back or push your back and take it? Do you linger believing to yourself that individuals should treat you better and that things should always go your method, or do you get out of your convenience zone and expand your circle of influence? Are you confident enough to go out and attempt, and sometimes stop working, to get your requirements satisfied or do you sit by the wayside waiting for the scraps of life and love to be given out to you? What have you done recently to expand your capacity for problem-solving and managing disputes?

Well, if a woman senses that you quickly give your power away to her, she may recognize that you may do it for another female. They may draw in women with all sorts of issues, whatever from mentally needy women to gold-diggers.

Depending upon how honest and simple you are with yourself while addressing those concerns, it might be time for you to KILL your Mr. Nice Guy Have no fear; I'm here to assist you through the process since I've learned how to murder my own Mr. Nice Guy consistently whenever he chooses to appear. Yes, it will make you uncomfortable, but that's just the point. Do not worry; I'll walk you through it.

How to Stop Being a Mr. Nice Guy.

The thing you ought to do is to learn the traits of a good man and end up being utterly mindful of when you or some other guy is acting like one. Find out to end up being mindful of your behavior, as this is the initial step to changing the ineffective way you react to people, specifically women.

The second action is to become honest with yourself and analyze yourself to see which of the good guy qualities apply to you the most. It's unlikely that you're a complete pushover when it comes to your relationships, as most good people tend to be at different points on the right guy scale. Figure out which habits are nearly automatic to you and catch yourself in the act.

As you interact with individuals, specifically women, take notice of yourself and what you state and do to prevent disputes and fight. See yourself in the act of doing the good thing instead of the ideal thing and start to choose the harder path consciously. It will make you a much better guy.

Instead of taking a great way out, challenge yourself purposely. Make an effort to get out there and get your requirements met.

Keep in mind to use common sense in this regard. You're not attempting to be disagreeable for disagreeing sake. If you disagree, you need to have a valid point to make, or if you're asserting yourself, then you ought to be attempting to get your needs satisfied without infringing upon the rights and wellness of others. Do not be embarrassed to request what you desire or to have a firm opinion about something.

Always take a look at the chance as a possibility to develop your self-esteem and assert yourself. If you consider it as a discipline or a practice, you'll be comfortable when you fail from time to time. But on the other hand, you'll also realize that with each mindful effort, you're getting much more powerful as a man. Always bear in mind that the practice of frustrating individuals to be authentic with yourself and others will strengthen your borders.

And even though the thought of individuals not liking you might tempt you to take the right way out, just keep in mind that most of the time, when you do defend yourself and act assertively in your relationships, individuals will appreciate you. You will get self-confidence in the long run.

- Stop Living for a Woman's Approval.

If you're presently living for a woman's approval, you're probably not one of the happiest people around. Every day that passes and you seek a woman's support, a little bit of your inner manliness passes away. You end up with a deep-rooted feeling of powerlessness and suffering, and you're too contrasted with doing anything about it. Or possibly, you're just unaware of what's going on inside of you.

As a man, you were indicated to be self-reliant, independent, and extremely capable of leading yourself and your family in the best way you perhaps can. When you go about your life seeking the approval of women, you end up losing these qualities. You wind up providing up your rights as a male, and for that reason, you'll find your life heading in a direction you never meant it to.

How to Stop Seeking a Woman's Approval by Becoming Comfortable with "NO."

The most valuable thing you can do for yourself right now as a fully grown male who wishes to become a much better guy for the lady you want is this: Become comfortable telling people "NO," and hearing "NO" from others.

Truthfully, if you followed simply this one piece of suggestions, you my pal are on your method to a much happier and productive life not only with women but also in every other relationship.

No is a fantastic word. It's a great thing. And yes, I know we live in a world that promotes stating yes to life and having a favorable psychological mindset, but stating no to others, to yourself, and hearing no and becoming comfy with it will make you feel a lot more powerful and in control of your life.

Learning to be comfy will assist you to overcome the concept of requiring the approval from other individuals. It's most likely the fastest method to become a more fully grown, confident, and self-assured man. You'll discover how to focus on win-win solutions in your relationships, and your ability to influence others will increase exponentially.

Make no error; the only way you can help others is if you are devoid of their approval. It's impossible to assist someone if you require them to like you authentically. You can't have both. So discover to become extremely comfy with people NOT liking you. Among the very best ways to do this is to end up being a no-man yourself.

Why Telling Her "NO" Makes Her Happy.

An intellectual woman is much more drawn into a guy who knows what he is and wants determined to get it. She admires and respects a man who follows his inner convictions regardless of what others may think. When she needs to hear it, she'll happily follow a guy who can inform her no.

A lady, understanding that she can sometimes be an emotional and unreasonable creature, will unconsciously desire a man and desire who can put her in her location when the time comes. Since it implies that you show courage and stability in sticking to your inner convictions, it's essential to her survival and to that of her offspring.

She'll understand that you appreciate yourself initially and foremost and that you're more than going to assert yourself and stand your ground if you feel as if your needs aren't being met or if your limits are being imposed upon. If you can defend yourself, she'll understand that you can defend her as well.

The more self-respect she sees that you have for the satisfaction of your requirements, she'll also understand that you'll be more than capable of satisfying her own. For her to see this quality, you should REFUSE to be a doormat for other people, including her, by asserting yourself. If you desire to become the kind of guy that can both attract and keep a high-quality lady in your life, timidity will get you nowhere. You need to have guts and iron nuts to say NO.

The second step is to become fully honest with yourself and analyze yourself to see which of the excellent person qualities apply to you the many. It's not likely that you're a total pushover when it comes to your relationships, as many good guys tend to be at various points on the good guy scale. Knowing When to Say "No" to NO and "Yes" to YES

When you discover a female that you're interested in, and you're getting to understand her a bit more in a dating relationship, think of saying no as a way to qualify her for higher access to more of you.

Do not merely offer her everything she requests for at the start. The word no ought to be used to communicate your limits, which you just let individuals have access to more of you (your intellect, your time, your social circle, your feelings, and so on) when you discover them reasonable to your values and standards.

When to say no and when to say yes, as you develop a meaningful relationship with a woman, it's essential to understand. It's all about balance and understanding the significance of being clear about what you will or will not tolerate from others. To become intimate with another individual, you need to want to compromise and jeopardize.

Constantly keep in mind that such things are best done in a relationship that is based on shared regard and commitment between two people.

If you can keep a positive attitude, stick to your weapons, and keep moving forward, every no will help make a much better guy out of you.

CHAPTER FIVE

The Three Kind of Men

The Beta Male, "Nice Guy."

When I was maturing, my mama, aunties, and other older ladies always told me that to get a girlfriend; I would need to be a good man. I 'd require to continuously buy a girl flowers, offer her presents, and take her out to eat.

" Wow," I believed, "I'll require to have a truly great task so I can have all that money to invest!".

Suddenly it prevailed knowledge that to be successful with women, you required to imitate an asshole rather than a good person.

I attempted that advice out and discovered that when I acted like a jerk, some women reacted to me more.

So I took a challenge looking at the men who were successful with women, the ones who weren't, and the ones in between, and I found out that there are three classes of men.

At the bottom of the list are the good guys, who make up most of the male population. The good guy is a guy who generally pleads for sex. He appears at a female's doorstep with flowers, drives her to an expensive restaurant, and buys her filet mignon with great white wine.

And you need to know what's paradoxical here? Think it or not, women consider nice people to be manipulative.

It's quite apparent to the lady why the great person buys her so many things. "They're just after something!" is a common mantra that women duplicate about nice guys. Nevertheless, she thinks he may potentially have excellent relationship potential.

And when sex does come, it's a substantial event, and the woman makes a huge offer about it. Hopefully, the guy does not have a high sex drive, because he won't be able to get sex whenever he desires.

Why don't good people succeed? The problem with the great man is that not just do women consider him manipulative; they also see him as boring. The good man talks about sensible things like diplomacy or how a cars and truck engine runs. In some cases, he boasts about himself and just how much cash he makes, suggesting that he can buy things for the lady. "How lame," she thinks.

Taking part in rational discussion and trying to impress a female with your smarts and earning capacity is a mistake that 99% of men make. Since it interacts neediness and low worth, it kills a female's attraction for you. You would not be trying to impress her if you weren't seeking her approval.

It snaps her out of her trance. So refrain from discussing that short article on Chinese trade policies you read in The Economist until you're socializing with your male buddies.

You need not pretend to be some type of moron around ladies. Women find it attractive when a person is a specialist in something. A guy who's an expert is automatically an alpha male. Simply make sure to mesmerize her with the knowledge you share. Don't bore her.

Women just want to have a good time, as the tune goes, and the good, dull guy isn't enjoyable.

The quickest and most convenient way to eliminate any destination a lady might be starting to feel for you is to feel insecure about yourself, or to be needy, or to seek approval. When you have the frame of mind of being desperate to please, you wind up coming on too strong, too early. You become clingy. It's like you're begging.

The Problem With Being Her "Friend."

Have you ever went for being buddies with a girl orbiting around her as the months' pass, hoping she will eventually succumb to you? Great deals of men do this, particularly the shyer ones.

These men end up functioning as emotional tampons for women. They listen attentively as their female friends inform them about what jerks the real men in their lives are.

Women just merely don't like spineless men for more than good friends. And when you imitate a good person and follow the woman's plan, and accept her to make decisions, she does not respect you.

And that's why the great guy doesn't get laid. Like I stated, women don't like to take obligation for sex. You, as the man, need to take that obligation and lead the method. That's what women desire you to do, and believe me, they love it when you do!

Being overly interested in a female's ideas and feelings is a waste of time because the bottom line is you can't control what a lady believes or feels. You can only control yourself. Rather of taking women too seriously (which offers them power over you, making you needy and unattractive), just see them as conventional sources of enjoyment and satisfaction in your life. That's it.

Next time you're with a woman, attempt to state "no" to her eventually. Saying "no" can be useful for women. Do it in a soft method, like this:

Her: "Let's go see a movie."

You: "No, not now. Let's enter in the next hour."

If she sees you as a difficulty, then she will be excited by you instead of bored.

If you state YES to everything your lady suggests, then she will quickly be saying NO to you, and in the worst place of all, the bedroom.

The alpha male is amazing to women because his happiness comes from within, so he does not burden her with any duty for his psychological state.

Let me state something here: your inner state is essential with women. For them to see you as adorable, you have to love yourself first. You have to have enthusiasm for your life, and you've got to go for what you want.

There are a lot of good guys out there who are down on themselves and insecure. That's why when it comes to love, great men do complete last.

The Jerk

The excellent person makes the fatal mistake of attracting their logic, whereas the one good idea the jerk does is to appeal to a woman's feelings.

Because they get women turned on by being so persistent and then going for the lay, jerks get laid. They are sexually aggressive, unlike the good people who are sexually passive. While the jerk creates unfavorable emotions within women, a minimum of them still creating feelings, rather than the great man who bores women.

Such women often act insecure and weird when it concerns relationships, so they're not the kind of women a well-adjusted male would wish to opt for in any case.

The bright side is that there is a higher level of men yet, whom I call the alpha males, who cause positive feelings within women without any genuine negatives.

The Alpha Male

In society, alpha males are the leaders; individuals look up to them. The alpha male is positive, socially dominant, outgoing, fun, a leader, safe and secure in himself, has high self-confidence, and is a guy who has his shit together.

When a lady states something sarcastic, the beta male gets angered, while the alpha male laughs about it since he understands women resemble his silly little sis. Studies of social scenarios have revealed that dominant people will mark their area in numerous nonverbal ways, such as using up space with their bodies, using a louder voice, controlling conversations, and using strong eye contact. Individuals around the alpha male tend to get sucked into his truth because he's intriguing and makes them feel comfy.

Since he isn't needy, the alpha male doesn't feel possessive or jealous over females. He also does not smother women by putting them up on a pedestal. Because of this, he understands that any female would be fortunate to have him, so if any specific lady doesn't opt for him, then that's her loss, not his.

On the other hand, the beta male fidgets, have low social status, is usually a follower instead of a leader, feels typically privately resentful, has low self-confidence, and is clingy and desperate with women.

I used to be beta. I was depressed and resentful. I desired a girlfriend because I thought having one would make my life worth living.

Six Beta Male Behaviors To Avoid

Here's something you may not understand about us people: we're wired to attach more weight to negative details about somebody than we do to positive details. That's why you can be having a great discussion with someone, and after that, all of a sudden, you change your mind about them.

So, because one wrong move can shoot down 100 great ones, it's crucial to avoid unfavorable habits that are characteristic of low-status males, or betas, if you do not desire women to treat you like crap and lead you on. These beta attributes to prevent are:

1) Seeking approval by ending sentences with, "isn't"? These concerns tacked onto the completion of sentences make you sound weak-willed.

2) Trying to dominate. Instead, just do it. Have a stronger mental reality and mindset than anyone else.

Presume individuals are there to follow you since you are the man.

3) Being belligerent, either with women or with other men.

The alpha male can stay calm under pressure and walk away when he needs to. Beginning a battle is a sign that you're a man with low status. Battling to acquire the affections of a lady is the supreme type of approval seeking, which decreases your attractiveness. With that said, however, if some person violates your limits and starts shit with you (like let's say you get bullied), there are occasions when you need to stand up for yourself.

4) Following the other person's schedule and discussing what they want to talk about, even if you find it boring.The alpha male just discusses what he desires to. Enjoy any alpha male in action (e.g., Politicians and CEOs), and you will observe this phenomenon. When an alpha male is bored, he does not conceal his disinterest. Do not offer individuals your attention until they've earned it.

5) Trying to mislead individuals and show that you're smarter than the individual you're talking with. You discover that the best leaders are safe enough when you look at leaders in business boardrooms or governor's mansions.

6) Checking out every pretty girl you see. A guy who's getting laid left and right doesn't have time for this, so you should not, either. See how they start examining you out and wishing to show themselves to you.

If they are a natural leader, alpha males presume the mantle of leadership as their birthright and act. They don't care much about what others believe. They do their own thing and do not seek approval.

While the jerk develops negative emotions within women, at least they are still producing feelings, as opposed to the great man who tires women.

The alpha male does not feel jealous or possessive over women because he isn't needy. Because of this, he knows that any female would be lucky to have him, so if anyone particular woman doesn't go for him, then that's her loss, not his.

And when you speak with a lady, lead the discussion. Mesmerize her attention.

As you deal with your habits, you will likewise work on adopting the mindset of an alpha male. The first thing I see that all alpha males have in common is that they assume individuals will follow their lead.

Be a catch to all women, Act as if pussy is no big deal to you because it's not a massive offer to men who get laid all the time. Act as if all your manly desires are entirely natural. You have no reason to excuse or conceal your libido the way good people do!

Be positive: Success originates from confidence. Presume you will be successful, and your mindset will increase the odds that you will. Presume that you are tempting to women.

Be brave and effective: At the very same time, be natural and enjoyable. Be a bit of a bad boy; however, don't be a jerk. If you want, have a devilish smile on your face.

Do what you please in life: Be real to your feelings. If you do not desire to do something, then don't. Be truthful with yourself. Be your own man.

CHAPTER SIX

Get Rid of Non-verbal Cues that Scream You Are Non-dominant

What do you think is something that makes a man most appealing to women?

You convey your dominant male status merely by acting the method dominant men do, by knowingly managing the nonverbal cues you send, thus developing the impression within a lady that you are alpha.

This technique is called the association principle. Within the mind of a female, you're associating yourself with desirable manly qualities while dissociating yourself from undesirable "nice guy" qualities.

Similarly, you can use impression management to control what the woman thinks about you.

What's supremacy? It's social power, which originates from assertiveness. As you go through your procedure of self-improvement, eventually, you will internalize the concepts of this book and become an alpha male.

Right now, you're going to discover how to imitate an alpha male, giving the impression of dominance by using your voice, your eyes, your habits, and your posture.

Your eyes are the primary nonverbal cue that tells individuals you're an alpha male. A dominant male is not afraid to gaze straight at individuals. By averting your gaze, you communicate submissiveness. When you look down, you interact with self-consciousness, shame, and a sense of low status.

Research studies have shown that using a soft, peaceful voice can produce the impression that you aren't assertive.

When you speak, attempt to let your words circulate and do not be afraid to speak your mind. People who hedge and hesitate are perceived as less powerful than those who do not.

Enjoy your habits and quirks. Attempt to avoid the following non- spoken indications of beta status:

1) **Using "ah" and "um," partial sentences, and partial words.** Research studies have revealed that individuals think about others who talk like this to do not have self-confidence and not be too brilliant. It's a sign of anxiousness. The factor we say "um" is because we're scared we're going to be interrupted by the other person. Instead, do not be afraid to stop briefly for impact. Stopping briefly previously essential points will make you seem more proficient, and individuals will remember what you say.

2) **Speaking too fast.** This produces the impression that you feel anxious and have low confidence. A regular, comfortable speaking rate differs within a moderate range from 125 to 150 words per minute. Decrease!

3) **Speaking with a monotone voice, also understood as mumbling.** Individuals with a narrow pitch range are deemed unassertive, uninteresting, and not have in self-confidence. So differ your pitch, and you will be viewed as outgoing and alpha.

4) **Pausing too long before responding to a concern**. This shows that you're thinking too hard for your response, which makes you appear indecisive. It likewise looks like you're trying too difficult to win the other individual's approval.

5) **Holding your hands in front of you**. This is a protective gesture. Instead, hold yourself open and vulnerable because you feel no fear.

6) **Twitching your fingers or hands.** When you're throughout the table from someone, there's a natural inclination to have fun with sugar packages or straw wrappers with your fingers. Do not. And don't drum your fingers on the table, women dislike that.

7) **Touching your face when you talk.** This suggests that you believe too hard, you're indecisive, or that you feel shy. To communicate self-confidence, hold your hands together in a steeple shape in front of your chest or face. (A lot of teachers do

this when they are lecturing.) When you need a substantial display of self-confidence is holding your hands at your hips, another posture that will help you. Police officers do this.

8) Folding or crossing your arms in front of you. On unusual celebrations, it is possible to fold your arms in an alpha style (watch Brad Pitt in the movie Fight Club for a great demonstration of this), however as a general rule, avoid it.

9) Rigid or stooped posture. An alpha male has a relaxed posture, whether he's standing or sitting. Relax and expanded.

10) Looking down. The alpha male holds his head high. It reveals enthusiasm. Looking down at the flooring telegraphs "loser." Keep your chin up. Expose your neck-- don't worry, no one's going to choke you! Take a look at the individual you're speaking with; remember what I stated about utilizing your eyes.

11) Nervous facial gestures such as lip licking, pursing your lips, jerking your nose, and biting your lips. An alpha male has an unwinded face and mouth because he fears nobody.

12) Excessive smiling. Studies of primates have revealed that beta males will smile as a method to signify their harmlessness to more powerful males. Beta human beings smile to reveal they're not a threat.

13) Walking quickly as part of your regular walk. Rather, walk a little slower than typical, nearly as if you're swaggering. You're alpha-- no one's chasing you, and you're not rushing to please anyone else. If you're not in a rush to get someplace, walk like you're unwinded and positive. Think: "I am the male. I can make any woman delighted.".

14) Walking just with your legs. Don't hesitate to move your torso and arms. Attempt this: walk as if you 'd simply had massive success and felt on top of the world. Enjoy what you do with your body. You might discover yourself moving your arms together with your shoulders and having a minor bounce in your step. Now, do that all the time.

15) **Slouching**. You do not have to stand annoyingly ramrod straight, but you need to have your shoulders back.

1) **Blinking a lot**. Slightly blink your eyes slowly. Do not close your eyes in discomfort. Simply let your eyelids unwind. In reality, let them sag a bit. Do not be bug-eyed.

17) **Moving your eyes back and forth when you speak.** That's extremely beta. Look at the other individual's face when you're in a discussion, and you're doing the talking.

18) **Holding too much eye contact when the other person speaks.** Non-stop eye contact makes you look needy, socially slowed down, and, honestly, like a weirdo. Rather let your eyes blur and after that gazed at her eyes. Look through her rather than at her. From extensive screening, I've discovered that looking at a lady about two-thirds of the time is optimum. By the way, just hold the gaze when she's telling you something genuinely intriguing. Otherwise, concentrate on other things like her breasts, her hair, things going on around you, etc.

19) **Being uneasy with your eyes.** The bottom line is that your eyes ought to be comfortable, relaxed, assertive, and sexual.

20) **Looking down or to the side before answering a female's question**. Look up to the team if you do require to look away before responding to think. Studies have revealed that this shows more confidence.

21) **Being afraid to touch a female, and thus being non- touching**. Be positive about it when you feel women-- any anxiousness at all can be fatal for your relations with her.. Be gentle if you use extreme pressure, you reveal your insecurity. (Since

you're alpha, obviously she will follow you, so there's no requirement to be anything besides spirited and tender.)

22) **Turning your head quickly when someone desires your attention**. Instead, use the movements that you would when you're at mouse sluggish and relaxed. You're not at anybody's beck and call. You're alpha, remember?

23) **Using long, convoluted sentences**. Alphas keep it brief and to the point.

Don't feel bad if you inevitably slip up and utilize some of these nonverbal cues from time to time. No one's best, so don't beat yourself up about it, especially when you're talking with a female. Let it go and keep the discussion moving.

When you consider such things too much while talking, you begin to question yourself, and when that happens, you feel insecure and distressed and become reluctant. Instead, just deal with staying nonchalant yet genuine at all times.

It's adequate to simply understand how you interact non-verbally with everything you do, since knowing ways you will start to avoid unfavorable communications far more.

Nine Nonverbal Cues That Say, "I'm Likable."

I've currently listed non-verbals that convey dominance. There are some great overlap deals of those signals, such as sustained eye looking while you speak that communicate supremacy likewise makes you more likable. Often dominance signals (such as leaning back) can make you more distant.

Be conscious of the following quiet strategies that magnetically get a girl to you:

1) Lean forward when you're sitting throughout from someone who is informing you something. This communicates interest in what they are stating. It's crucial to make sure that the female is highly interested in you before doing this, given that leaning back is a way for you to play "hard to get non-verbally." Lean forward to offer the impression that you're easy to talk to when she's interested in you.

2) Directly orient your body and face towards her. Note that you should have supremacy established before doing this, because you lose supremacy by being more direct with your body language.

3) Smile.

4) Have a relaxed and spread-out posture.

5) Dress similarly to your group, but simply a bit cooler than everybody else. If you meet the gown expectations of individuals you engage with, you will be much better liked.

6) Wear lighter-colored and more informal clothes. (However, such clothes likewise interferes with your viewed dominance.).

7) Maintain shared eye contact, go on and look into her eyes, and she will like you. Do not do it more than 70% of the time, though, as stated previously.

8) Make sure your speaking voice is enjoyable, expressive, unwinded, and interested in what is being discussed.

9) Do away with any facial expressions that are not pleasant, an absence of gestures, looking elsewhere, closed body movement, and an uncomfortable-looking posture.

Once again, make sure to strike a balance between dominance and likeability. If you never smile, then the female won't like you. However, if you smile excessively, it makes you appear like you have low social status, you're trying too hard.

Some things, such as an unwinded, spread-out posture, help you with supremacy and likeability, so you should be spread out and relaxed all the time. Your eyes are the number one nonverbal hint that informs individuals you're an alpha male.

CHAPTER SEVEN

Women Want Men That Other Women Want.

Women enjoy men that other women are into. This phenomenon is called preselection. You know how a man strolls into a club with a female on each arm and, all of an unexpected, every other girl is considering him.

And no, this isn't a case of mistaking correlation for causation. Studies have found the same thing: Women are intuitively drawn into men that other women want.

Get a picture of a man, show it to some women, and the women might or may not be drawn into him. Program the same man with a stunning female (or women) and all of an abrupt; he is quickly viewed to be 10X more appealing.

On a final note, this only works if attractive women preselect you. Having some fat uggo chasing after you will have just the opposite result.

When women know that other attractive women desire you, you become 10X more beautiful in their eyes. Now, let's take an appearance in ways you can apply this to your own life.

How To Use The Power Of Preselection.

You may not (yet) be able to take the common alpha male technique of appearing to constantly have a few hot women with you, or strolling around with women hanging off your arms, but that doesn't indicate you can't effectively use the power of preselection to your benefit.

Here are a couple of easy methods you can get going utilizing the power of preselection.

• Post images of yourself with some adorable girls onFacebook. 'Nuff stated.

• Date more women. Remember, dating is not unique. You can date as lots of women at the same time as you like. So date lots of women-- it'll increase your attractiveness in their eyes. You can also integrate this idea with the next one,

● Be vague about your relationship status. If a girl asks, do not state you're single, simply say something like, "It's complicated," and say no more. You might likewise make things even murkier and more mystical by using words such as "girl" and "girlfriend" interchangeably.

● Don't expose your notch count. If a woman asks you how lots of women you've been with, just say something like, "What, today? Few ..." or "If I told you, I 'd have to eliminate you.".

● And more! So get creative.

Nice guys love to invest as much time, effort, and money into women as they possibly can. They incorrectly assume that the more they invest in a woman, the more attraction she feels for them. A bad young boy spends just enough for a woman to rationalize being with him. When you eliminate your inner-nice man's excessive eagerness to please others (especially women), you'll discover individuals (specifically women) progressively seeking your attention and eager to please you.

A man's physical attractiveness plays a far smaller sized function in a woman's attraction than a lady's physical appearance does for us people.

Be Exciting, Mysterious, and Unpredictable

We humans naturally have a minor inferiority complex. You see a hot girl, and you imagine her as the most fantastic, remarkable person ever to live. You picture her living a crazy, amazing life. You feel insufficient by comparison.

In reality, though, hot chicks live very typically, uninteresting lives, similar to the rest of us. That hot chick you felt frightened by? She is most of the time, very bored. She lives a boring, regular, mundane life.

And just as we men frequently view hot women as being too awesome for us (even when they're quite uninteresting and common), so too do women. Women do this to a far, far greater level. That's why women are intensely drawn into dark, strange men. They build up this great fantasy in their mind, something that no truth might ever wish to match.

This is likewise why frequently the very best sex you have with a girl is the very first time you bang her; she's trying her best to please this mysterious alpha guy. However, as you become increasingly more familiar, and she starts to understand increasingly more about you and recognizes that you don't have any other options (i.e., other women wanting to bang you), the sex becomes plain. Dull. Common. She puts less effort into it and desires to have sex less regularly. She goes from eagerly trying to please you to "just tolerating" you. Eventually, you wind up in a sexless marital relationship, and, if you're fortunate and she doesn't have a "headache" for the twelfth night in a row, you may get enthusiastic, once-a-month starfish sex.

This never occurs to alpha males. They (whether consciously or automatically) realize the power of maintaining an air of mystery and unpredictability. They understand that girls regularly forecast an aura of mystery around men that they know really little about. Moreover, they assume the very best.

Don't spill the beans. Do not inform her everything about you, be unclear, cultivate an air of mystery, and let her complete the spaces with her creativity. Be a mystery, man.

The Power Of "Busy."

Do you think high-value alpha males have time to relax with some chick all day? No, of course not. They've got better things to do.

You see, for a lot of 'good guys' make the mistake of assuming that if only they were better if just they could invest more time with a chick, text her more, speak to her more, and go on more shopping journeys with her, then she would be brought in to him. Sadly, not so.

Stay busy. That which is limited is important. If you spend too much time with her, she will inevitably take you for granted.

Crucial Ideas.

1. Tell her less about yourself. Let her fill out the spaces with her imagination. Looking for to impress her only leaves her not impressed, and you discover as needy as if seeking validation or attempting to compensate for a perceived inadequacy as if you feel you're unsatisfactory for her.

2. Spend less time with her. That which is scarce is valuable. Investing every extra minute with her and continuously flooding her with messages ends only in her not valuing you and taking you for granted.

3. Be unpredictable. The unpredictable is amazing and launches dopamine (the brain's satisfaction chemical). Being completely unpredictable, mesmerizes women even more than merely being a dull old foreseeable Joe Blow. Shake things up!

Tease Her.

For example, if a girl asks a great man if she looks fat in a dress, he'll desperately inform her no, that she looks fantastic and gorgeous. If a girl asks an alpha male if she looks fat in a gown, he'll react to it as the dumb concern it is, telling her it appears like she just gained 400 pounds and must take that dress off right away together with her panties and then provide her a wink.

He's not her shoulder to sob on nor her psychological tampon. He's not there to put her at ease and inform her how "fantastic" she is. An alpha male is there to have enjoyable and entertain himself, nothing more, absolutely nothing less.

Don't hesitate to (playfully) give women shit and tease them, especially if they ask/say something downright dumb (e.g., "Do I look fat in this?"). Don't put women on a pedestal. Simply treat them like the typical, boring, farting, pooping individuals they are. Above all, entertain yourself and have a good time.

When you put a woman on a pedestal, all she can do is look down on you. This is a mistake that so numerous people make. They attempt to be so good, do good things for her, go out of their way to impress her, and prioritize her joy above their own.

As if she is the higher-value person, and you're simply some low-value man attempting to offset your inability by being additional significant and continuously looking to impress her and win her approval.

When an alpha male just treats her like a normal person or, in some cases, as if he is the higher-value one, as if he is the prize-- by teasing her, playfully poking enjoyable at her, tinkering her and ruffling her feathers, he discovers as being much greater worth. The lady will look to impress him and win his approval rather than look down on this poor 'good guy' attempting so difficult to win her love.

Here is the major difference between alpha males and good men (likewise referred to as beta males) when it comes to women: A beta male imitate she is the prize. An alpha male acts like he is the prize.

And guess what? Women are hypergamous. Women never want to be the reward. They desire him to be the reward. That's why you hear women discussing how Mr. [X] is "a real catch." Women are biologically hardwired to be brought into men that they feel transcend to them.

Put her on a pedestal, go out of your method to impress, and constantly flex over in reverse for her, and she'll see you as an unattractive, inferior male. Treat her like a normal individual (or take it an action further and imitate you're the remarkable one) by playfully teasing her and providing her a great ribbing from time to time. She'll see you as an attractive, exceptional male. As if you're the reward, not her. And that's what she desires.

Women Love Ambitious Men.

Alpha males do not do this. They have more crucial things to do, whether it be building a service, pursuing an enthusiasm, or founding an empire. They live interesting, daring lives by themselves terms. If they like, they may permit a lady to tag along for the trip, but women are just a device to live, not life itself.

Discover something that thrills or even consumes you, an objective, a greater purpose, an enormous objective-- and aggressively pursue it.

Women don't desire to be your life; they want to belong to it. They want to tag along with a guy as he sets about living an interesting, adventurous life. They do not wish to be the center of his life, his primary focus. Alpha males deal with women, not as the centerpiece of their life, however, as a device.

Here is a quick recap of the alpha male traits and

CHAPTER EIGHT

Flirting Skills that Comes Naturally to Women and Emotion

Teasing.

Women tease with their eyes, looking flirtatiously at guys, and then they move in so close in preventing their glance. They tease with the way they dress, using clothing that exposes so much, but not excessive.

Consider how strippers get you delighted and after that withdraw, get you thrilled, and then withdraw.

Women do this all the time, on a variety of levels. Because they recognize that foreplay begins long before you reach the bedroom, and women do it.

Tease a lady playfully, since she loves it. Tease her about :

- Her responses to your questions.

- The way she gowns.

- Her mannerisms and peculiarities.

Slap her in the ass when she says something bratty. Ball up a paper straw wrapper and toss it at her, with a mischievous smile on your face.

Frame the entire interaction with a woman practically like you're her big brother, and she's your humorous little sister. Keep everything lively and amusing.

Her Attraction Signals.

The reason is that if a female is staying speaking to you and being enjoyable, certainly she doesn't dislike you! But it's always possible that she likes you just as a friend (though unlikely as long as you keep pressing the interaction forward), so my advice is to learn and memorize the following list that I've developed, and after that, try to forget it.

The following list remains in no particular order.

1. She compliments you on almost anything.

2. She feels nervous around you. Look for indications of anxiousness, such as her muscle jerking.

3. She teases you playfully.

4. She makes an effort to inform you just how much she likes the same things you like.

5. She speaks about things that you both can do in the future. "You like vintage clothing stores too?" she may say, "We ought to go sometime!" By the way, this is likewise something you should raise with girls. Do not make it too major. (Say anything playfully unreasonable that the two of you might carry out in the future. Keep it verbally non-sexual naturally.).

6. When her legs are crossed, look at the foot of her leading leg. It is an indication you've got her full attention if it is pointed toward you.

7. When it lulls, she makes an effort to keep the conversation going. Once in some time, you can even test her destination by purposely allowing the discussion to stop briefly on your end (See if she restarts the discussion.).

8. She touches her face. When an individual touches his or her face, it's a sign that they're thinking of something.

9. She gazes into your eyes and holds her gaze.

10. She stair at you. (Being passive by nature, women will follow the lead of a male they feel attracted to.)

- Adjusts the rate of her voice to match yours.

- Matches the pace of your breathing.

- Laughs together

11. Stroking around things such as a wine glass or pen up and down with her thumb and guideline finger. This suggests you have a strong result on her, good guy!

12. She tosses her head back or side-to-side. View her hair to sway as she does it.

13. She touches her face while taking a look at you.

14. She dangles her shoe off her foot or even takes it off.

15. She rubs her fingertips around her upper chest.

16. She rubs her palm on the back of her head, triggering her hair to fluff out.

17. She plays with her hair while looking at you.

18. She shows an authentic smile instead of one that's forced.

19. Because her pupils are big and dilated, her eyes sparkle.

20. She raises her eyebrows sometimes.

21. Her nipples are solidifying. Of course, you can only identify this if she's wearing the ideal clothing.

22. She has an unwinded face. (However, sometimes a non-relaxed face can be fine, such as when a female is so brought in to you that she feels nervous.).

23. She focuses all her attention on you, even when there are other individuals around.

24. She touches you while speaking to you, even if it is "accidental." Women are highly mindful of their bodies, so it will rarely indeed be an accident when they touch you.

When she laughs at one of your witty statements, look for her to touch your arm to highlight a point or brush her foot versus yours.

25. She chuckles at your remarks as if they're the funniest things she's ever heard, even if they're just mildly amusing.

26. She reveals her tongue, like when she touches it to her front teeth or licks her lips.

27. With her body turned towards you, she unexpectedly sits upright, with her arm muscles tensed and her breasts pressed out.

28. She shows her palms to you. Open palms indicate she feels open with you.

29. She rubs her wrists or plays with her bracelet.

30. Her skin ends up being flushed. Look especially to observe whether she blushes. (This can also be a signal that she feels horny.).

31. She rubs her earlobes or plays with her earrings.

32. She asks you questions about yourself. They will not simply be the shallow questions that she 'd ask anyone (" Where are you from?"), however instead will be deeper questions to learn what makes you tick (e.g., "What are your enthusiasm in life?").

When a lady acts bratty and asks you some concern like, "Why did you decide to talk with me?" or "Do you say that things to all the ladies?" the very best thing to do is to not look for the most elegant response.

Instead, the best method to respond is with indifference. That method you remain in control of the frame. (Whenever you appreciate what a girl believes, that provides her the control.).

There's never a requirement to feel as if you need to captivate a female. Doing so makes you beta. Communicate with her when you converse with a woman. Screen her to be sure that she can keep a conversation opting for you. That makes you the alpha male.

As you constantly presume the female's brought in to you, the most crucial rule for keeping control of the frame us to always be ready to stroll away.

Although I discuss perseverance until you either get declined or laid, sometimes it's good to be the one to stroll away very first (if it's a girl you do not like), just to understand that you can. If a female views a guy as an obstacle, that keeps him compelling. It indicates she has to work for him, and if she acquires his affections, that's her benefit. Suppose you're ever a "sure" for a lady, that offers her validation and triggers her to lose destination for you. If you merely assume attraction, that ensures that the lady continually believes that she's more attracted to you than you are to her.

CHAPTER NINE

What Women Really Want from Men

The ancient question that has actually been asked by men all over the world is this:

What is it that women want from us?

To be honest with you, the answers are limitless. Since there are billions of women worldwide, they all may desire different things. Being the human that we are, there are certain things that both women and men desire that, for the most part, are non-negotiable.

These are the integrated needs that emerge from both our primal desires and our human nature. For that reason, it's important to frame the question of "what women want?" based upon a female's primal desires and requirements. Why? Well, it's because the answer will always be the same for each woman. Focusing our question on human nature and impulse will produce a bit more consistency in figuring out precisely what is that quality, a lady wants from a man.

So to simplify things a bit, the question that men need to ask is this:

What things do women want from men that can be thought about non-negotiable, universal, and primal?

Now that we have the RIGHT question, let me give you the RIGHT response:

The main point that a female desire from a man is the experience of feeling like a lady. She desires to lose herself in her womanhood, and the only method she can handle this feminine experience is when a man imitates as a guy.

Seriously, women are feminine creatures by nature and intuitively desire to be treated as such, no matter what society may state. It's the natural order of things, therefore the more feminine a lady probes a man, the more comfortable, secure, and desirable she will feel. It is this experience of feeling like a creature of feminine appeal that women these days are yearning for from men.

The lady of your dreams is yearning for the kind of man that can make her feel like a woman. And she has no option, however, to respond to the man that can activate this sensation within her.

This indicates that by establishing the sort of manly qualities of character that a female is Hard-Wired to respond to, you'll naturally make yourself alluring and irreplaceable to her.

The Masculine Character and Women

The more masculine a guy is, the more feminine he will make the women around him feel. And the term masculine, in this case, refers to a male's character and his habits. The best method for a male to develop a more manly disposition is to go about constructing his character and enhancing his character purposely.

Simply put, as a man, you need to take control of your life, take duty for your ideas and actions, and find out to handle your emotions effectively.

If you wish to impress a female, or rather, the perfect kind of high-quality lady that you wish to bring in, the very first thing you need to do is concentrate on building your character and making yourself far more masculine in a natural sense.

This is the only crucial thing you can do in this life. Nothing is more appealing to a quality woman than a man who places a high worth on things like sincerity and integrity, and other qualities of a sterling, noble character. And while physical strength does count for a lot in stimulating a female's physical attraction, keeping her drawn in over the long-term means that a guy should also have the strength- of character.

A lady wishes to know that she can be sure of her experience with you. She would like to see that she can depend upon you while times are excellent. She desires to be confident in your ability to handle temptation if you're faced with the chance to do something questionable to acquire something you desire. In these circumstances, she wishes to be sure of your stability, as she hopes that you won't do something that doesn't align with your beliefs just to earn a profit or enjoy a minute of fleeting enjoyment.

This is VERY crucial to her.

On the other hand, a woman likewise wishes to know that she can rely on you to deal with disputes when times aren't so good. She wants to be guaranteed that she's with a MAN through and through. When things are going well and then fall apart at the joints when a dispute arises, she does not want to feel as if you might just be simple. You'll wind up looking like an inexperienced little boy, and trust me, that won't be a fun experience for either of you.

A woman would like to know that you can make her feel preferable, safe, and secure, womanly, and gorgeous. She would like to know that you're the type of man she can grow with, one who can help her grow and reach her complete capacity as a female. And the more masculine you remain in character, the simpler it will be to make her feel in this manner naturally.

And when it pertains to the romance department, the manly man is a heroic and irresistible fan to his female. He knows how to meet her both physically and emotionally, and he makes it his responsibility to ensure that her deepest needs for physical and psychological intimacies are regularly fulfilled.

How to Build a Powerful Masculine Character.

Character building for a male is maybe the most important task he might ever carry out in his life. I know it was and still is, for me at least.

As soon as I began to concentrate on changing certain aspects of my character, I started to see the outcomes in my life change too. And think it or not, the sort of life you lead and the sort of woman you'll draw in and keep will all depend upon who you are as a male.

All of your lead to life will be based on who you are at your masculine core. Your train of idea, your automatic responses to situations, and how you handle disputes and other individuals are all connected to your character. Women are much more attracted to a guy's character and character than by his appearances, accomplishments, or belongings. Much more so, premium, smart women, those with more experience in handling men, tend to have a fundamental ability to see a guy for what he truly is on the within, regardless of the halo effect created by his physical look or the material representations of his high-status.

Fortified with this understanding, it is of best interest for you to focus on the advancement of your character and personality.

This is just a beginning point, however for the sake of helping you to get your feet wet, here are a few manly character-building tips:

1. Start a brand-new severe pastime, something that you can see yourself ending up being truly great at. This will build your strong self-confidence, and it will also assist you in establishing discipline as you develop your ability and increase your knowledge in a brand-new way.

2. Develop a brand-new ability or an old skill and use it as a method to get ahead in your career or perhaps build a service. This will assist you in taking conscious control of the self-development procedure by forcing you to hone your psychological faculties to be imaginative in your work.

3. Travel with your woman frequently and strategize extraordinary experiences with her. Take the effort and make it your company to guarantee that her life is filled with romantic fun and adventure.

4. Set a challenging goal for yourself and devote yourself to attaining it. This will help you to build character and will reveal your female that you are goal-driven and enthusiastic.

5. Sign up with a health club or sports team or get a martial art and develop your body. This is critically important.

Why? Since physical strength and martial guts are two qualities that have been considered absolutely "masculine," in its purest essence, throughout human history. And although it may not look like it, establishing your physical strength and increasing your capacity for martial nerve also assists your character development. Pursuing such activities will increase your male confidence while at the very same time, making you much more physically attractive to women on a biological and primal level. It will also assist you in developing self-discipline and proficiency, as ending up being skilled in any kind of weightlifting, sports, or martial arts will require fantastic amounts of effort and persistence.

6. Find out more books that will propel you forward in life. Any book that will help in your advancement (like this one) will help you to construct a more compelling character by sharpening your psychological faculties and your ability to fix problems.

7. Discover some buddies that will assist you to stand out in life. Sign up with a social club where men collect and find methods to include worth to the gathering and your community. This will assist you in growing in character as you are forced to learn how to relate much better with other men to get your requirements fulfilled and the needs of others by working together.

8. Come up with fun and creative methods to reveal your affection on an on-going basis. This will assist you in establishing the virtues of love and appreciation, as the more you pour yourself into the relationship, the higher benefits you will enjoy.

9. Be proactive. Offer up recommendations to resolve disputes, be the very first one to make a move, and take more initiative. Discover to end up being a skillful decision-maker. This will assist you in developing the skillful quality of personal initiative.

10. Go above and beyond the call of responsibility in your love life and establish your manly resourcefulness in your relationship. Discover what makes your female tick and ensure that her requirements are satisfied even before she recognizes she had one. This will help you to establish the habit of going the extra mile and over- providing on your pledges and commitments.

Those ideas ought to be sufficient to help get you started.

Even though they're all pretty helpful suggestions, you've got to do the work. Start with something and commit to seeing it through. Do something about it now, and obstacle yourself. This is the only way to construct the strong character that you desire and the manly qualities that the female of your dreams will require in order to submit to your management. Keep in mind, cultivating a strong, manly character is essential for any male who desires higher success and relationship happiness.

Basing our inquiry on human nature and impulse will bring about a bit more consistency in figuring out precisely what it is that a quality woman wants from and in a man.

The Key to Her Heart: Earning and Keeping Trust

A woman can just love and respect you as a male as far as she can rely on being with you. It's as simple as that, my friend. Above all else, she needs security from you.

This is why women have the habit of testing men, day in and day out. It is a subconscious practice that is constructed into their mind. When it comes to earning and keeping her trust, since of this requirement for certainty, a woman will continue to check a man throughout his life to ensure that she can rely on him during the bad times and even the excellent times.

Now, you must keep in mind that these tests aren't truly indicated to trigger any unwanted tension or to bring drama in your life. They are implied to keep you on your toes and to "persuade" you into being a better male or at least into being a guy, duration. For a woman, testing you will reveal to her the difference between who you state you are and what you're made from.

Checking you enables her unfiltered access to the true nature of your character, as she assesses the places in which you lack congruence.

Initially, it might be simple for you to get by on a charming personality alone. Under a wise woman's testing, any façade you may be attempting to present to her will not hold up over time. You can be as charming and as dashing as you desire, but in the long-run, your real character will expose itself. More experienced women are familiar with this, and they'll keep testing you until the "real," authentic you finally presents himself.

Her Experience with You

What a woman wishes to be sure of more than anything is her experience with you. This exceeds her physical senses in that she desires to feel secure with you in mind, body, and soul. When the going gets tough, she wants to know how you'll deal with her psychological nature, and she wants to know if she can rely on you.

What she truly wants is a feeling of security, knowing that no matter what life throws her way, you'll exist as a source of strength and encouragement. She desires to feel safe in your capability to weather the storms of life.

The factor for this is because a lady is naturally hardwired to seek out power and security from a male to endure, as ending up with a weak, fluctuating, or predatory man can significantly endanger her presence.

This is why an intelligent, top quality lady will not only be extremely brought in to a male with a strong character; however, she'll end up being extremely bought a man who has ambition and drive. Without this certainty, a lady will not be brought in to you, or if she discovers that you're incapable of making her feel safe and secure over the long-lasting, she can not stay drawn into you.

CHAPTER TEN

The Secrets of Being an Irresistible Catch

The trick to acquiring and maintaining the love, admiration, regard, and desire of a quality woman is to progress into a much better male continually. As an intellectual man, you must never stop growing. You should never stop developing knowingly. As a guy, you ought to always be seeking the next level, a much better paradigm, and a more excellent perfect as you live your life.

I might probably sum up this entire book with this one concept: Women are brought in to men who illustrate the characteristics and qualities of leadership. An excellent woman will stick to a trustworthy man and follow his path of leadership. Her love, regard, and desire for him will continue to grow so long as he can captivate her mind, body, and soul by making her an irreplaceable partner in his grand adventure.

An excellent female desire a guy who can lead her, one who can make the hard decisions. She desires a man that can gain her self-confidence, and she desires him to take her for who she is and to love her deeply and romantically.

To keep her mesmerized, you need to progress. Your dedication to on-going personal development will mesmerize and amaze her continually. Your desire to enhance yourself alone is a turn-on for her merely because women are designed to be our indispensable equivalents.

What does it take to establish a fully grown character that will captivate an excellent female for life?

What does it require to have that masculine sensation of power that just comes when a guy takes obligation for his life and pursues his own course?

Let's dive in and discover out, shall we?

- Take Responsibility for Your Life

People don't provide you responsibilities when you're a guy. Even if they are "required" upon you, you will not have the ability to carry out at your greatest up until you "take" it upon yourself.

Leaders take responsibilities; they do not wait on it to be offered to them. Taking responsibility is the first and most crucial to consider as a man's development if he wishes to rid himself of the whiny little young boy inside of him. A guy must discover to avoid blaming individuals and situations for his results and must take full responsibility for his whole life instead.

Learn to take ownership of the choices you've made. Accept the truth that you are where you are in life since of the decisions that you've made, which the outcome of your tomorrow will be based on the choices you make today.

If your personality attracted her, but you still maintain the boylike attitude of blame and playing the victim, she'll quickly find herself losing her desire for you.

- This is a slow and agonizing death.

To take duty in your life, very first accept whatever the way it is. No matter what your life looks like, just accept it as the outcome of your choices and begin planning ways to improve it. This will bring you much assurance and a much better sense of control over the future results in your life.

- Discover Your Path and Never Stray from It

A male without a clear course in life is merely wandering through the world aimlessly and with no direction. No excellent woman in her right mind is going to desire to come along for that ride, a minimum of not for long.

Understanding your purpose and following your distinct path in life will provide you a deep sense of what it suggests to be devoted to something larger than yourself. It will give you an inner voice and belonging that will encourage you to make favorable modifications worldwide around you.

It will become your fixation, your mission in life to fulfill this purpose. You will live a much happier and successful experience as soon as you've found your purpose and choose to stick to your course, no matter what.

Having this special course will make you a lot more effective in the world and a lot more attractive to the right woman who can assist you in the accomplishment of your life's goals.

As long as you make your mission the essential element of your life, you'll never have to worry about losing the desire of the right lady merely because she will end up being extremely interested and invested in you attaining what you set your heart on.

And as soon as you know what your function in life is, you'll discover that it is easier to have peace of mind when things do not constantly go as you've planned.

Naturally, discovering your path may require some deal with your part. It will take some effort in self-reflection and some soul browsing. Trust me, it is worth it in the long-run.

- Quit Consuming and Become a Producer

No, this has absolutely nothing to do with films, music, or end up being the next Rick Rubin or Quincy Jones. This has to do with ending up being an incredibly productive creator, contractor, and company in your family, community, and your piece of the world. One of the key things that separate the mature man leader from the average Joe is that one is a manufacturer, and the other is a consumer.

The average Joe takes in more than he offers to the world in terms of worth, but leaders provide more than they get in terms of worth. The manufacturer will always be greater than the consumer. Absolutely nothing is more evident in the lives of fantastic men than the reality that they were men who found out how to develop and offer huge amounts of worth in their communities. They used their imaginative resources to build, pioneer, construct, and produce new and important things.

If you wish to grow and reach your greatest capacities on your own, your lady, and your neighborhood, you should end up being a prolific manufacturer. The path to male management needs that a guy abandoned his childish methods of believing to establish a mindset of prolific imagination.

Through the efficient management of your time, cash, and resources, you can improve your levels of efficiency and imagination to add more value to the world than what you draw from it.

- Master Your Fears

Two main fears can obstruct a man from achieving success in not just his relationships, however, in any area of his life. These two things are the fear of failure and the worry of criticism.

A leader discovers to overcome these fears by mastering his feelings. He understands that failure is simply a step on the course to attainment, and that criticism is simply a sign that he is alive and doing something rewarding and productive with his life.

You can not prosper in any way if you can not fail forward. And if you do not discover how to handle criticism, then you will not be able to do anything that matters to anybody.

To master your worries, you must master your feelings. You can do this by changing your concept about failure itself.

- Failure is rarely irreversible.

Instead, see it as a stepping stone and a lesson found out. See it as something you MUST go through to accomplish success.

When it comes to criticism, if it's positive, simply see it as a method to enhance what you're doing. If you're too attached to what you're doing, unfavorable criticism can only harm you.

Instead, find out to love the procedure of becoming instead of being solely concentrated on the result. If you can do this, you'll hardly ever need to worry about criticism from others.

A leader does not need the approval of others, consisting of women. However, if he's in a healthy relationship with the best lady, he will seek her counsel when the time calls for it. However, otherwise, he is self- approved most importantly, and this displays in the clearness of his thinking and the powerful outcomes of his decisions.

Mastering your fears will end up being more comfortable as you end up being a much better male. As you grow into a complete understanding of who you are and what you're capable of, you'll have a greater comfort when dealing with the lots of unknowns in your life.

As a guy, you need always to be seeking the next level, a much better paradigm, and a greater ideal as you live your life.

A good lady will choose to follow and trust a man who is knowingly following the course of leadership. A male must find out to prevent blaming people and circumstances for his outcomes and ought to rather take complete obligation for his whole life.

Ask several men you know what their path in life is, and most of them most likely can't provide you a concise and clear answer. A male without a clear course in life is just wandering through the world aimlessly and without any instructions.

- Cultivate Masculine Courage

I can provide you no much better guidance for attaining success in your relationship with your lady and other areas of your life than this:

Challenge yourself purposely and regularly every day of your life. This will construct the most important particular found in ALL excellent leaders and highly successful people of society. It will develop your guts.

We've most likely covered this a lot of times already; however, it can not be stated enough. A guy's courage to do what is right, to follow his course in life, to defend what he believes in, and to be the very best variation of himself is his most preferable and appealing quality to a female.

Courage can only be cultivated by purposely doing it. Courage is something you "DO" It's not something you believe about. It's an action you TAKE. A guy can develop systems of his guts by doing the essential things he's typically averse to doing.

I think that self-confidence is merely the way we communicate our levels of guts to others. It's impossible to have one without the other. Intellectual and physical courage is incredibly important; it is ethical courage that is especially important to a female.

Ethical courage will provide you the strength and ability to exercise all of your other virtues. It will assist you in making the best decision no matter what others may think about you. This is among the most necessary elements that separate the typical man from the man who leads others.

The guy with terrific quantities of courage is not scared to state what needs to be said and to do what should be done. And any lady would be more than ready to put her confidence and rely on such a guy.

- Accept Yourself Now

It's fantastic how I'm about to cover everything up with this last piece of suggestions viewing as though your mission is to become a better male for the lady who's right for you. It may appear inconsistent, but believe me, it isn't.

You MUST discover how to accept yourself for who you are and for where you remain in life beginning today. Although your mission as a mature man is to develop and reach your greatest capacity continuously, if you fail to accept yourself and discover contentment in your present phase of development, you will not be reliable in becoming the best version of yourself.

All change begins with self-acceptance. You should discover to acknowledge your present value in the present state you're in because if you do not, you'll continuously prevent yourself whenever you disappoint your development objectives and individual vision.

Forgive yourself magnanimously every single day. Provide yourself a break for Pete's sake and decline to berate yourself for any factor whatsoever.

Stop stressing over what other men are doing and remain concentrated on what is right for you at your phase of development and advancement. Become a master at self-acceptance by being grateful for what you have.

Master the art of revealing gratitude in your everyday life, and your life will change drastically.

Here's a life-changing suggestion: if you don't take anything else from this book (which I doubt), and this is the only thing that you find out, you WILL delight in better relationships in every area of your life:

Cultivate the practice of being grateful for your life just as it is today, and how you 'd like it to be in the future. Make it a HABIT to see the favorable side of things, and develop a positive personality towards life. Program your gratitude in how you live your life and EXPECT good ideas to occur to you.

And yes, it is possible to turn into a more positive and capable guy while being content with who you are right now. Just concentrate on your strengths and the important things you like about yourself.

All it takes is a determination always to pursue the very best, balanced with the decision always to forgive yourself rapidly whenever you do fail.

A great female does not desire an ideal man per se; she simply wants a guy who's ideal for her. The simple truth that you've devoted yourself to her and a path of constant personal development is all that she needs to appreciate, regard, and remain in love with you for as long as you want.

- Continuously Seek Wisdom

I 'd much like to end our talk with one final piece of advice:

Don't be afraid to get great guidance that can help you to enhance yourself and your relationships.

Now, if you've read this book, then you undoubtedly don't have that problem, but this is just a pointer. Too frequently, we decide to follow a particular path thinking that we've got it all found out or that we'll simply "go with the flow."

Although going with the flow can be enjoyable, there's nothing more encouraging than knowing your side as your guide. It's better to be prepared in any situation, no matter how much you think you might already know.

Good ideas just began to change in my love life when I started to seek out excellent guidance and use it. Some of it was free, some of it I paid for, but in the end, it was all worth it.

As men, we can be a bit stubborn and prideful, especially when it concerns getting this location of our lives dealt with. Nevertheless, when a male decides to arm himself with a bit (or a lot) of knowledge, a whole new world of possibilities begins to open up for him.

When it concerns his relationship with his perfect lady, the more he educates himself, the better he ends up being to her.

So remember to keep knowing and to continue your advancement path towards developing as a man. It'll make your romantic life much richer and more satisfying in the long-run. Do this, and the best lady will see you as a tempting catch, the sort of male that she 'd rather not live her life without.

CONCLUSION

Before you go, I 'd like to state "thank you" for getting my book. I understand you could have selected from dozens of books on comprehending women; however, you bet on my guide, and for that, I'm exceptionally grateful. Thanks again for checking out all the method to the end.

A man can build systems of his nerve by doing the things he's generally averse to doing. Physical and intellectual guts are essential; it is ethical guts that are especially important to a woman. This is one of the most vital aspects that separate the typical male from the male who leads others.

Remember to keep on knowing and to continue on your advancement path towards maturing as a male. Do this the perfect woman will see you as an irresistible catch, the kind of male that she 'd rather not live her life without.

HOW TO FLIRT WITH WOMEN: HOW TO APPROACH, FLIRTING, TALK, ATTRACT, DATING AND SEDUCTION WOMEN

LOVE ACADEMY

INTRODUCTION

This book is not about getting you more texts coming from girls. It's certainly not about that, because I do not assume that's what you yearn for. I don't assume you desire to be as bright as you can be in your texting. And I don't assume you would like to make her fall for your text messages.

I believe what you want is to be capable of getting her to say YES when you ask her out or ask her to meet up. That's precisely what this book is about.

The book is most likely to challenge a few of the most cherished conventional beliefs on "good texting." If a few of these challenges I toss your way make you a little uncomfortable, that's good. What I want you to accomplish when that takes place is to take the empiricist's perspective and say, "Okay, let me attempt it."

Your intuition might point out, "She would certainly never do that," but often, your intuition lies when it comes to trying something new.

The emphasis here is not to build your ego unnecessarily or fill your head with platitudes. Instead, the main objective of this book is to get her off the phone and on a date with you.

CHAPTER ONE

How to Text a Girl

Your Objective in Texting

Let's begin with the fundamentals and strategy of texting ladies. This is what will effectively drive how you structure your messages and how you view texting generally.

Most text messages from men have a slipshod approach: they text girls without any definite aim. It is not sure just how they expect objective-free and direction least ext messages to achieve much.

This book will shine a little light on texting and get you in the right direction. You will ever have two objectives when texting, and they ought to never overlap. Here are the common objectives in texting ladies: (1) Build rapport and comfort, or (2) Set up a meet.

The number 2 (set up a meet) is your core objective. And the rapport-building or comfort-building you do in #1 must remain in operation to make to 2 a reality. Beyond that, these two objectives are the core.

It has been observed that a lot of men that text has a kind of pseudo-objective... like "keep texting her, then fish around in some way to get a date."This awful, atrocious quasi-objective leads men to send all sorts of half-baked text-- messages that leave a girl staring at her phone and asking herself, "Why the hell is he texting me this?" All these types of texts do is torpedo a guy's efforts towards getting the girls interest. Thumbs down for the pseudo-objective. If you are one of those who do that, stop it now.

When you send text, a woman should recognize right away what your objective is. And if you remember the two goals earlier referred to, they are: (1) build rapport and comfort, or (2) set up a meet. You want her to be capable of telling straightaway what the text is all about. The reason you wouldn't want any overlap is that as soon as you mix date demands with chit-chat, it becomes messy. That is when you see a guy fish around as he builds rapport, seeking for some way to transition into asking her out. Do not fall into this trap; Keep your objectives distinct. Either you text her intending to build rapport, or you text her to set up a meet.

Don't beat around the bush. Don't text without any objective. Don't send lots and whole lots of content. Don't get too wordy. Be straightforward and direct. Do text with your goal in mind. Do send a handful of strategic texts. Be concise and accurate. You should regularly be trying either to build rapport and comfort, or set up a meet.

Cold Texting and Warm Texting

It's essential to understand the distinction between cold and warm texting. When you text a girl that is thinking about you or even expecting to hear from you at the time you text her, that is warm texting. While cold texting is when you text a girl that is not in any way thinking about you or even expecting to hear from you when you text her,

Why the distinction? Given that you're going to adjust your tone to match exactly how prepared she is to talk to you, I'll give you examples:

First, envision, you're off to meet a male colleague for lunch. You're friendly with him but not very close. He sends you a text: "Just parked my car. Grab a table yet?" This may be the first text he's sent you all time, but it feels normal because you anticipated hearing from him.

Let's now imagine it's 10 am the next day, and you are busy with some work you don't like doing. You'd rather be back in bed. Then, you receive a text coming from that same coworker, which reads: "Just had my second cup of Joe. How's your morning?" To an exceptionally social individual, it could be trendy to receive this text ... however, most individuals will find this intrusive and strange. They will wonder, "Why did he text me? What does he want?"

That is the difference between cold and warm text messages. The first one-- where you considered to meet your coworker-- was normal, since you needed to know when and where to meet. The second one, though-- where would that originate from? This isn't a guy you're very close with. Is he making an effort to become buddies with you? Does he desire something from you? Does he have some form of a crush on you? Those are the type of confusing questions that would stand out in your head when a crisp text isn't structured right. Structure it inappropriately, and it can quickly appear like it just happened from nowhere.

Proper Ways to Structure Your Texts

The moment you send your first message in anew text conversation, there are a few elements you often would like to feature. For our purpose, a new text conversation (with a cold text) begins whenever the old conversation reaches a natural end. No exceptions, regardless of whether you only spoke to her via the phone. This is still a new conversation, even if you just changed channels.

The components to include in a new text conversation are: (a) Greeting, (b) Her name, (c) a new relevant information, and (d) something that presents consideration for her.

Each of these plays a major role in the "real feel" of the text. Below's what a complete first text along with all the features look like:

" Gabby, hello. Running a bit behind, sorry; it will certainly be there closer to 2:30. Still cool?"

We have:

(a) The greeting: "hey" (b) Her name: "Gabby."

(c) Some info: "Running a bit behind"-- "will be there closer to 2:30" (d) A little bit of consideration: "sorry"-- "Still cool?".

The fact that you texted to let her understand you will be late in the 1st place--that also counts as consideration.

In certain instances, we can quickly lose the greeting, and it still feels fine, mainly if the text is warm and comfortable. Therefore in the example above, we can drop the greeting (hey), and it is still fine because she expects you to deal with logistical issues in the run-up to the date. Often, though, you will wish to include the greeting-- it improves the possibility you'll get a positive response.

Next off, you should always use a girl's name in the first message of a new text conversation. This trips a mental trigger that assures her that you're speaking to her. Text, phone, and email don't just feel that person when you do not use the other person's name.

Exclamation points and emoticons have a lot more upside than downside. They'll add more benefits to your text and help compensate for the absence of body language, voice tone, etc.

If you make use of periods, your message will appear like this:

" Hey, Jim. I hope your week has been perfect. Seem like mine's never going to end."

If I get this type of message from a girl, It makes me think the girl's a downer; she appears whiny, and I get worried that if I meet her, she'll drag me into negative topics or even she'll get clingy and too dependent if we meet.

Surprisingly, some researchers have found out that people rate text that ends in periods, like the one cited above, as a lot less sincere than text messages without them.

Now, compare that earlier message to this:

" Hi, Jim! I hope your week has been perfect:) Feels like mine's never going to end..!".

Doesn't that feel fresher, energetic, and stunning! I can not wait to meet this girl. The same message, with different punctuation at the end of the sentences, She's likely to be a breath taken. Our text messages (as men) will not be that bouncy since we won't be texting just as ladies text, but it'll be related.

Texting is just one of those mediums from which you've to choose. In this instance, the choice is between masculine and negative or feminine and positive. I'll go for feminine and positive and count on my real life masculinity to plow under any kind of worries of my text being too adorable. Despite these features, texting still feels more natural than face-to-face communication. You can not much afford to do without them and go through a lot more unnatural feeling.

One more point to keep in mind on text messages is grammar. How grammatically correct should you be?

The challenge with regards to grammar is becoming loose enough to look informal, but positively not careless that you appear ignorant. Individually, what this means will vary by subculture, nation, continent, and age. I can't tell you precisely what syntax to use because it might be the wrong grammar for your age or where you reside! I will say this, though: your aim with grammar needs to be making your text persona match your in-person persona as much as you can.

Text works better as an extension of the person. Hence, if you've acquired an incredible office works and you suit up correctly and appear to be good, you won't wish to text her:

" Wat up bae, would u like to eat some food with me?"

Even though you're the local crack dealer, you yearn for cleaner grammar than this. Usually, a slang is more challenging to understand, and the more complicated your texts are to understand, the less she will go through and answer them. Don't forget, mental loads. Casualness as a stylistic choice is indeed excellent; going too far into way too much shorthand is all you should avoid as much as possible.

Thus far, we've talked about greetings, syntax, names, and punctuation. Next, we will discuss the other two elements to feature in every new text conversation: Information and Consideration.

The relevant information you discuss is the "point" of the text; it's the main reason why you texted. The consideration is the "bond" in the text; it's your duty to show consideration and care for this girl.

You should make true feelings when you text her because without that, you're weak. If she is baffled about why you sent the text or she thinks that it's cold, you aren't focusing much on her (lack of consideration), she'll have unpleasant feelings with regards to the text correspondence and be less likely to respond favorably.

The relevant information could be:

" Stuck here in this serious gridlock ... this town has the worst traffic!".

" Had the most delicious shrimp of my life last night ... I may still taste it.".

" Thinking we just have to get together soon.".

The consideration can be:

" How's your week looking like?".

" How was your test?".".

 What's your schedule for today?".

I also advise you use something like, "What's your full week looking like?" That's because I find it a fantastic, open-ended question to:

(a) get a girl to chat just about anything fun, different, or fascinating going on in her life, and

 (b) put together avenue for us to meet up.

Below's what our text to these girls should look like:

 "Hi Lily, hope your weekend was great =) Sitting here in gridlock... this town has the worst traffic ever! How's your week looking?"

"Jane, Good morning! I had the most tasty shrimp of my life last night... I can still taste it. How did your test go?"

"Hey, Mary! Thinking we need to get together very soon. What's your schedule looking like this week?"

These are trendy, lovely, and personal, and will often get you the expected response. How she gets your messages is influenced partially by the preliminary perception you made on the girl you're sending out messages to, obviously, and also partially by precedent (for instance; if your first perception was bad for whatever reason, or if you've now set poor criterion in your correspondence where you text her, but she disregards your text, a first message now might be somehow too late), but usually, structured in this manner, you'll often get a response from women, and also they'll practically be at the very least slightly warm in their replies.

Ways to Text a Girl and Build Rapport.

It is recommended that you send an introductory text to a woman one to four hours after the initial meeting with her. If you met her towards the end of the night in a bar, at the nightclub, at a party, or on the street, one or two hours later is fine if you're practically heading to bed.

This introductory text is to break the communication ice systematically. The importance of this is that you want her to get comfortable interacting with you... but don't forget that you aren't attempting to know her this way.

The catch with communication comfort is: the longer you wait, the much more unpleasant the first contact will be (whether via a text or phone call). Send a text within one to four hours so as to protect against any awkwardness or anticipation settling in. This means you establish rapport via text message as soon as possible.

All you are expected to do to break the text ice is send a basic message like:

" Glad to come in contact with a fellow traveler -- -Frank."

or

"Delighted to meet someone like you tonight---Tommy."

So you give her:

(a) a goodwill statement to let her know you're glad you met her,

(b) a smiley face to share warmth and lovely feelings, and

(c) your name.

The above works as follows:

It helps build rapport. You've quickly moved to develop rapport via text and eliminated clumsiness or anticipation. When you send a text or make a phone call later, it will be a lot more natural.

In some cases, men take a lady's phone number and act unpleasantly or never message or call at all. A woman can become fearful with regards to whether you like her or intend to get in touch another time. If it appears you maybe like one of those Jekyll/Hide men who are cool in person yet scary over text, send her a good (short)statement with a lovely smiley, and you'll eventually set her mind at ease.

It gives her your name. If you've been at this for quite some time, you will develop an ability to remember everybody's name, since you get so used to meeting many new people that it simply becomes a normal part of you. Yet, most girls are not so skilled, and they may well forget your name no matter how much they like you or just how much you relate with them. This can downright embarrass a girl that a lot of times, she can not speak with you for the shame of it. Put your name at the end of that initial message, and you can get rid of the likelihood of her feeling stupid or ashamed.

To build the desired rapport, you may end off that first message, and not contact the woman at all the following day. You can later send a few rapport-building messages to make her comfortable talking with you.

Some basic tips on rapport-building texts include:

Be concise. Shorter messages get even more responses than long ones.

Remain Positive: Nobody cherishes a downer; bring considerable positive energy to your messages. Ladies must eagerly anticipate messages from you. Make them dread messages from the boring, life-sucking men ... while you illuminate their days.

Maintain it to a couple of messages. Unless you enter an incredible text conversation with a girl, you'll wish to keep it to about three to ten messages sent, generally.

It's alright to differ your response times, but do not reply a woman's texts too quickly than she responds to your own up until you make much progress, lest you risk looking like you're waiting by the phone for her reply with nothing better to do

How to Arrange a Meet Up with A Girl Through Texting

If you wish to build comfort and rapport with a woman, you can adopt a rough schedule like this: (a) preliminary message some hours after you first meet and collect her number; (b) rapport-building texts two days after the very first meet/number collection; (c) fix the date four to five days after the very first meet/number collection.

You do not need to speak to her for weeks before she's all set to meet you; you don't have to win her over. You just need to get her out.

There are three aspects to a meet-up message: (1) Be warm, (2) Ensure you offer value, and then (3) keep your eye on the ball. The ball being the eventual meet up..

The value you provide can be something loving or romantic with her, or it might be leading her to what she wants to do (which is to meet you). Don't get distracted.

Here's an example of what your conversation might look like as you forge ahead toward setting up a meet:

You: Jane, hi! Let's fix a time to grab a bite. Exactly how's this weekend looking like for you?

Her: Sure! This weekend is beautiful. How are you doing?

You: I'm good! Why don't we make it this Saturday at 2 pm. We can meet at Main St Avenue Exit 3 and go from there. Is that Cool?

Her: Okay!

You: Great. See you on Saturday!

That's all it takes. Keep in mind that when she asked how you were, you didn't give room for any distraction; you remained focus on the goal(the meet up). Remain focused and keep pressing for the meetup, smoothly, carefully, and smartly--. Plan a great date, and she's all yours.

The Three Common Texting Styles Used By Men
There are three forms of text messaging styles prevalent amongst men these days:

1. Clueless Boring Questions type of men

2. Endless Conversations type of men

3. Incredibly Witty and Interesting type of men

The above categories are listed in order of frequency, from the most to the very least experienced.

Despite being listed as the last, the Incredibly Witty and Interesting man is not all that uncommon.

Before we learn what to do to achieve good results with women out of texting, let's start with a consideration of what these three categories of men do, and why it does not work. Try not to be miffed if you know you're one of these individuals because if you are, you're precisely the target of this book.

Clueless Boring Questions type of men

To women, the most frustrating texter is the Clueless Boring Questions guy, hereafter abbreviated as CBQG. The CBQG has no clue on how to text women or what ladies would like to see in a text message. At no time has CBQG ever asked himself:

" If I was a girl, how would I reply to a message like this?".

He quickly assumes that all ladies are like him-- lonely and without many options. Thus, they must love to get messages from him, and they, therefore, ask clueless uninteresting questions like:

" What's up?" "How's it going?".

" How was your weekend break?" "What are you doing?".

" Do you have strategies?".

CBQG thinks that women enjoy getting texts like this from him. Besides, he 'd love getting texts like this from ladies. Of course, it must go both ways.

CBQG usually becomes distressed when ladies do not address his inquiries. He wonders why he does not get the desired rep. He thinks ladies are difficult to understand and unnecessarily make things complicated.

He doesn't stop to understand she isn't there in person and doesn't have the same level of context and expressiveness from him as she would if he was there.

The CBQG doesn't also assume to himself that: "Lame people inundate most girls all day with lame requests. Most guys message, write, and say to girls the same ineffective things often.

This never happens to him, because CBQG recognizes himself so well that he knows that he's not ineffective. He assumes that everybody else needs to know this, as well ... even if he behaves the same way men, who are lame do.

" She'll know I'm not ineffective, also if I appear ineffective," CBQG thinks. "Otherwise, she's shallow and not worth my time!"

CBQG thinks that ladies must recognize his inner awesomeness. Women need to hammer out the lameness he shows outside to find his awesomeness inside.

CBQG spends several evenings alone, angry, and confused by how the world can be so cold and so confusing.

Endless Conversations Guy

Endless Conversations Guy, hereafter referred to as ECGis usually a CBQG that tidied up his act. Someday he considered his phone, which was devoid of replies to the messages he 'd sent, and says to himself:

" If I were a woman, how would I respond to a message similar to this?".... and in an unexpected insight, he recognized he had been doing it the wrong way. ECG is, you might, on a much more informed level than CBQG. He realized the need to involve a woman in dialogue. And also, he's recognized women don't desire to address stupid questions.

ECG still doesn't get much further beyond "engaging her in dialogue"-- and there he's usually stuck. ECG's conversations tend to look something similar to this:

ECG: Hey, Shirley, how did your weekend break go? I saw some close friends on Saturday, but yesterday was all just relaxing.

Girl: Hey, it was beautiful. My buddy from out of town came to visit, so we went to some restaurants and also saw some sights ... that was all about it.

ECG: Cool, what sights did you see?

Woman: Oh, you know, he harbors, Sea World, just the usual things.

ECG: You know, I've been living right here for five years, and I've never seen Sea World. Everyone keeps telling me I ought to go.

Girl: I understand; I did not get to sight Sea World till I was 19, and also I grew up here. Isn't that ridiculous? But you should go, it's a lot of fun.

He doesn't know that the more time she spends with him in text chats and the less time she spends with him in person, the worse she feels about him, as researchers found studying young couples in 2014 (Luo, 2014). He doesn't realize most girls who engage in these with him are either (a) just doing it because they're also bored, or (b) just too nice not to send back a response. To him, it feels like he's unlocked the key to texting girls: just keep texting.

You can imagine how annoyed he becomes when a woman he's spent a lot of time within endless conversations always dodges his date demands-- and how perplexed he is to find, after weeks or months of discussions, that some other guy has eventually become her guy.

" How can this be?" ECG thinks, "I thought we had such special discussions!".He's bewildered ... it just does not make good sense. Why would she invest so much time talking with him and then decide to date somebody else?

The Really Interesting and Incredibly Witty Guy

Last but not least is the Interesting and Incredibly Witty Guy, henceforth referred to as RIWIG. Such a man is the next stage of evolution after ECG. He's a man who's discovered that endless conversations don't work. They can be tedious, kill his intrigue, and every man and his brother would engage in them fruitlessly.

RIWIG has a lot more experience with women than either CBQG or ECG. He does understand women react well to wit and choose interesting poor children to boring nice people.

" So," goes RIWIG's line of thinking, "what could be much better than being a poor boy via text?".

Most texting advice you'll see online or speak with close friends comes from RIWIGs. They've split the texting code, they'll tell you. They've identified just how to develop the feelings they desire in females ... wish, laughter, intrigue. Being really interesting and incredibly witty over text is the method of getting ladies drawn into you.

RIWIG leaves those guys in his dust. Just as CBQG can't hold a candle to ECG, ECG's odds to beat RIWIG in a text fight are about as good as a medieval pikeman's odds against a Navy SEAL with a minigun and a grenade launcher.

RIWIG's text conversations often tend to go something like this:

RIWIG: Oh, man, I just had excessive food. Never need to have eaten that last drumstick. Suggestions: gluttony doesn't merely make you fat; it's also quite uncomfortable.

Woman: lol ...where did you go, and why 'd you overeat?

RIWIG: Friend had a birthday party. There was far way too much to eat; I felt an ethical obligation to make sure there weren't unnecessary leftovers.

Woman: Did you save any for me?

RIWIG: Thought about it, but decided against it. You ought to be thankful I prevented you from withstanding a similar experience to mine.

Lady: But I want some too!

RIWIG: You know what, miss out on ... you are starting to get too hard now. The majority of ladies are a lot much more cautious when they claim things like that to me.

Lady: I'm talking about the food, duh!

RIWIG: That's what they always say ...

Girl: You are such a geek.

RIWIG: Hey, so [conversation continues]

This type of man is a big step up from ECG. But despite his extremely amusing and intriguing message text conversation, RIWIG is prone to some issues: (a) women will still frequently be dodgy about setting updates, and (b) when the dates are eventually fixed, the woman usually treats RIWIG as a prospect (i.e., she sets barriers to sex).

RIWIG thinks. "I was engaging, witty, sexy ... everything a woman looks for in a lover, not just a friend!

Being wittier and more enjoyable isn't the answer. The answer is something much simpler than CBQG, ECG, or RIWIG think it could ever be.

The Fourth Type of Texter

There's good news for the Clueless Boring Questions Guy, Endless Conversations Guy, and Really, Interesting and incredibly witty Guy. The good news relates to the fact that there's a fourth texter with a style they haven't tried out, thought up, or looked into yet.

And he doesn't need clueless boring questions. He doesn't require endless conversations. Heck, he doesn't even need to be all that interesting or witty. All you've got to do to use his style is be able to send simple text messages ... and tell the girl you want a date with her before you get her phone number.

If we had to give this kind of texter a name, I think it 'd be Just Get It Guy(JGIG). The style is more concerned about keeping things simple. The truth is, less "natural" media (like email and text messaging) are less meeting for people to deal with (Kock, 2004).

But a lot of guys still don't get it. They're still trying to mix in CBQG or ECG or RIWIG elements with this style of texting. Because those ingredients work great in other things you make, it's like taking a gourmet recipe and throwing in extra eggs and baking soda. The result is not something better. It's something worse.

CHAPTER TWO

Ground Rules for Texting

Text Messaging ABCs

The first step is to deprogram you from negative texting ways of thinkings, inadequate approaches, and misunderstandings.

These are things that make texting more challenging than it needs to be, causing men to send messages that simply don't work.

To do this, I'm going to give you the 8 "mental foundations" of texting you need to know. These foundations allow you to think about texting a woman in a reliable method that gets her ecstatic to see you and also all set to come out on a date with you.

#1: Faulty Models Are Your Responsibility to Fix, not women's.

You can choose to blame other individuals for your life, or you can head out and get what you desire. You definitely can't do both.

It'sblame and be miserable, or accept responsibility and go all out for what you desire.

As you go down the texting styles, you'll find out that the more advanced a guy's style is, the more he criticizes girls. The 'Clueless Boring Questions Guy' is the most awful. To him, nothing is his error.

The worse a man is with ladies, the more fault he sees in ladies. What's responsible for this phenomenon?

It's a symptom of defective psychological models.

Women give out phone numbers a lot. And they do not appreciate getting clueless monotonous questions from any person, even close good friends, family, lovers, guys, etc

So, simply imagine how a girl feels when she gets such questions like this from some person, she does not know all that well, or some guy she met in passing at the workplace or the bar or on the road or in class, even if he attracted her (in the beginning).

She would regard him as somebody who's a liability and not fun to have around. Her passion in him goes from whatever it was before the clueless monotonous inquiries began, right to absolutely no.

It's not ladies that are the problem. It's the texting style you have adopted.

If ladies don't think, act, or react the way you think they should, it does not in any way mean all the over 3.5 billion in the world need to change. What it implies is that your thinking pattern needs to change to suit the style women are.

This phase is about changing that version you've adopted.

2: Phone Numbers are Easy.

Inexperienced people view phone numbers as a big deal, which is one of the reasons they struggle so much with the concept of texting.

The problem is that, to girls, the phone numbers are not a big deal!

An inexperienced individual gets a girl's contact number, and it feels like an enormous success. Now he can relax. For all intents and objectives, he has found a sweetheart.

Except she does not see it in this way. For women, a telephone number is simply the START. And also, girls offer their names out regularly to individuals whom they never wind up talking with or seeing ever again.

You're not the only one asking her. Various other people ask her as well. And she says yes to several of them often.

Phone numbers mean nothing. They're nothing more than an opportunity. They are not a guarantee or an assurance of any kind.

If it assists, you can think about a phone number just as "Here's a way you can get me to meet you once more if you do a good work making me desire to.".

By doing this, when you start seeing numbers, you'll promptly start to understand why clueless uninteresting inquiries are a death penalty. That is, it's far much easier to say"No" to you over the phone than in the real world.

And if you're most likely to be boring and clueless on the phone, what's she supposed to do ... be delighted?

Giving out a phone number does not amount toa pledge; it's just a possibility.

3: Emotions Don't "Stick."

When you first exchange numbers with a girl, you could leave on cloud nine, dreaming about the fantastic future you'll have with her. Possibly you had an effective communication with her and genuinely connected with her on a quite deep level. Chances are, she's forgotten all about you.

Oh sure, she might still be considering you. You don't know that, and it's much better to think that she isn't. If she isn't, how then is she going to respond to your first text?

It's possible she's forgotten almost everything about you because it's more probable she's frustrated by other important issues in her life.

Is your message going to make her smile? Is it going to take a lot off her shoulders?

If I was truly angry and frustrated right now and I received this text arbitrarily from somebody I could barely remember, what would my reaction be? If the response is "a lot more upset and annoyed," you need to head back to the drawing board. Find something that much better stimulates the appropriate emotions.

Excellent-- that's a perk if she remembers you. You'll still send her a fantastic text, and she'll be even happier to hear from you. If she doesn't, if she's forgotten all about you and you eventually send her the right message, you still stand a good chance of taking her out on a date anyway.

4: People Want You to Help Reduce Their Cognitive Loads.

Envision you are anxious, you're worried like insane, running around trying to do a million things that you have pending. You wish to scream and punch the wall and pull your hair out just because you're so far behind on things. Then, you receive a random text message from some guy you met at a bar the other day who seemed like a nice person.

" What's up?" the text states

What's up??!! What, am I supposed to sit here and figure out what that means? Like, you simply desire to fire the crap, like I have time for that? Or, you want to ask me for some kind of favor, or want me to use something to you?

This happens to be the thought process of a very busy lady when she receives a text like that. It has been observed that ambiguous messages like "What's up?" are a few of the most mentally challenging messages of all. And that makes them amongst the least likely to get an expected response.

A lot of men want to get messages like this from women. Women do not appreciate receiving messages like this from men simply because such text messages raise mental loads.

The second a lady reviews a message like this; her mind puts whatever else on hold to ask itself: "Who is this? Is he going to ask me for something? Is he going to begin sending me lots of messages if I reply?

Much of the moment, her mind will just consider these and many other related questions and may just decide to put off her phone and never respond.

This is not because she's mean or cold or impolite or withdrawn or even indifferent; none of this is true. It's only because there is too much brainstorming to do, so she puts it off and then forgets about it. Or she remembers it once again later just to put it off once more.

Like it or otherwise, when it involves less-clear media like text messaging, the duty of making the sign of a text clear drops on the person sending out the message, not the one is getting it. It's on you to make it clear what you mean-- she isn't going to sit there and attempt to figure it out.

You should aim to be clear and make it very easy to respond to your messages. You must reduce mental loads as much as feasible.

Do not make her think. Do not make her wonder. Don't get her into giant open loopholes; she needs to invest substantial amounts of mental power on. That's an invite to overlook you, and you don't want her to see you as rude or socially stunted, either.

Smart individuals do not shift huge mental loads on other people using text. They make points easy. They take burdens off. You should, as well.

That implies, instead of "What's up?" you can say:

Hey Jane, I hope you had a great weekend. Mine was strong and restful, simply what I needed. When's okay for you to get hold of that sumptuous meal this week? Let me know when your schedule's clear, and let's fix it up.

No surprise what your motives are. No asking herself what you're after. No pondering on the best way to respond, and even if she needs to respond whatsoever. All she's required to do is tell you when her schedule is free or open.

It's very easy, and since it's very easy, you're most likely to get what you desire: a date!

5: You Must Not Take Your Eye Off the Ball

Think about it. How many of the terrific relationships in your life come from lengthy text message conversations? How many friendships? Sweethearts?

If you're like lots of people, the answer is this: 0.

That's because texting is an atrocious way to build purposeful relationships. This is not how to text ladies at all.

People still keep doing it. They do it in droves. And the reason for such is because their eyes are not on the ball.

If you've ever found yourself mired in lengthy text conversations, I bet you've never taken time to ask, "Where is this going?" And if you did, I'm sure your answer to that question would be "I have no idea!"

That is not the way to run a text conversation. It's not just how to run anything.

Imagine if a sailor takes out a ship into the deep blue sea with no clue as to where he was going. "I'm most likely to locate a gorgeous, unoccupied island available with a pirate's buried treasure, and I'm going to be rich!" he tells himself; "I just need to sail around sufficiently till I locate it!" After the triggers on his voyage, he might end up discovering an island in the vast sea with a few doubloons hidden in an upper body. It's much more likely he'll die at sea or return to port, bitter and more frustrated.

You practically always miss out on the mark when you shoot in the dark. With really couple of exceptions, texting is awful for building an emotional connection, getting involved in an actual discussion, changing a stranger right into a partner or fan, revealing your individuality and high qualities, or keeping or growing attraction.

You will certainly be missing the mark once more and once again if you use it for these things. You will not also get better at hitting the target in the dark. You'll simply throw away a lot of bullets, time, and patience.

No matter what happens, establishing a date should be the primary objective of your messages. Using it for anything else departs from your core goal and slashes the chances you'll ever make it to your aim of a phone call.

6: Girls Talk Because They Like to Talk

Unless you're exceptionally a talkative, I guess that you do not spend a good deal of time in long text talks with your male friends. Nor do you likely have these with a lady that's now your lover.

The majority of men just get into these long discussions with women they're pursuing. And such men assume that the girl understands what the bargain is. "So, once more, clearly she must know this, and also undoubtedly, her texting back to me is permission to continue with her!"

There're a whole lot of presumptions in there, and they're mostly inaccurate.

As socially sharp as many women are, they are incline visitors. They know you desire something when you message clueless dull inquiries or unlimited conversations or large quantities of really, intriguing, and extremely amusing stuff ... they simply will not understand what it is you desire.

Most ladies love talking! They will chat with you merely to chat. And they'll like it. Lots of girls will be delighted to message to and fro with you all day ... and not just you. They do it with their lovers. They do it with their friends. They do it with the other individuals that are chasing them and also texting them all day long.

You're there talking, thinking it's nearly in the bag, because she's so ready to chat with you. And she's there chatting with you, her friend, her lover, and other people.

This isn't the way to a lady's heart. It's merely a way to help her pass the day. You're losing if you invest time in long text discussions with women, and you will soon be much more useful as a texting friend than you are as a prospective lover.

CHAPTER THREE

Opening up the Hook

Now that you've got your structures established and you have learned the basics, you're all set to study the mechanics. These are the certain subtleties, the screws and nuts ... the core of how to text women and have it go the way you want it to, nearly consistently.

#1: Propose the Date Before You Ask for the Number!

It feels easier to ask for the number. If she says "no," all she's denying is giving you her phone number?

However, that's outrageous. If she refuses to give you her number, by extension, she refuses all future possibilities of you and her doing anything together, ever. That includes dating.

When you are trying to collect her phone number, you should request the date first! Not only does this make it much easier to get phone numbers from girls, it additionally makes things a lot easier when you identify how to correspond with her later.

Better still, it makes you look confident. If you had a chance to ask a girl out personally, then didn't, and waited to do it over message later, she may presume you lacked the guts to ask her personally and, therefore, not worth meeting again face to face.

If men began to ask women about dates before they asked for phone numbers, CBQGs, and ECGs would come to be extinct. And RIWIGs would end up being a threatened class.

All you need to do:

Her: [mid-conversation anywhere you meet] ... so after that, I entirely left there before things could get back at worse!

You: That's funny.

Her: I know. I thought I was going to pass away for a minute! That woman was insane!

You: Hey, I'm most likely to have to jet in a minute, but we ought to grab a drink or some food today or early next weekend. What's your routine like?

Her: Oh, I don't know, I'll have to have a look. I believe I'm free on Sunday.

You: Cool, I'll text you. What's your number?

Her: 619 ...

Isn't doing this much easier than the big issues most guys make from trying to get phone numbers?

Moreover, doesn't that make it way more straightforward when you wish to text her later? I believe you understand specifically what you need to do now.

As a suggestion, you may open your phone right now and erase every number you took from ladies you didn't ask out in advance. Or, if you'd instead try out something before you remove those numbers, text every one of them now with something like:

Hey [name], I just stumbled across this trendy little coffee shop in [area] with the most impressive warm chocolates. I intend to take you there - want to get hold of a chocolate and a snack with me sometime this week/ next week?

Any of the ladies you get "yeah, sure" or a " how about we do XYZ rather" from, hang onto; you can surely work with that. Anyone, you get a "no, I really can't" or a "sorry, I'm busy" from, simply delete.

Now you're starting fresh and every number you collect from now on, before you collect it, ensure you've collected it in the context of doing so in order to set up and plan for a date.

Say goodbye to figuring out what to message her—no more pacing back and forth in your room just to decide what you should send us a text.

Now, you surely know what to say: you're going to message her to figure out when she intends to meet you.

2: Use an Icebreaker Text.

The longer you wait after getting a girl's number to text her, the weirder it begins to feel. There are a variety of "weirdness" elements that enter into play: she questions when you're most likely to text her, or she forgets about you completely; plus you build things up in your head and get uncomfortable, or you push things off so long that she wonders why you're texting a week later.

Solution? You just need to break the ice.

Starting a conversation provides you the liberty to be more natural later. The awkwardness of wondering whether the discussion will certainly be comfortable and also typical over text is gone.

Starting a conversation sets the tone for you to message women later on without needing to introduce yourself or remind her of when she met you. That's because you built those initial feelings while they're still fresh in her mind.

A simple icebreaker text resembles this:

You: Nice to meet you, new friend: --- Frank.

or

You: Glad to have met you: --- Frank.

You do not tell her you "like" her, qualify her (as in "You're a cool/amazing/neat lady!"), ask her any question, or suggest a date.

You do keep it short, use the word "good friend," if possible, sign your name.

Since this is just to break the ice and comfort her, you aren't one of these people that's in love and creating her novels now; it's brief. You relate from the beginning that you follow the Law of Least Effort, and you show her that meeting a new woman isn't a big deal to you ... like it is for many men out there that are quick to deluge women with lots of messages following the meeting.

Since you wish to confuse and captivate her a little bit, you make use of friends where feasible. Do you like her or not? She assumes you do ... and now you're using this ambiguous term. Ambiguity is among the properties of text, and it's one you can resort to your advantage. You use this, and she's assuming ... she's intrigued. The majority of guys specify spoken passion right away and also kill the excitement, enigma, and intrigue. Women don't want men like that ... they want men that'll keep them presuming and that will not let them know how the story ends-- keep up till it does.

If a lady appears very into you and appears to see you as far more exceptional standing than herself, you might choose to drop "friend" ... so as not to send her right into denial, assuming she can't get you.

If you do not include your name, and she forgets it, she's either going to feel uncomfortable that she's forgotten, and not react, or feel embarrassed that she's forgotten, and have to ask you. This is an all-too-common reason women use to comb guys off if they're on the fence.

Occasionally, you will get a girl writing "Who?" back after your initial message, and if it's just a few hours later, and if you've authorized your name. This is generally a brush-off attempt; do not react back by telling her who it is.

When should you send out an icebreaker text? About 1 to 4 hrs after meeting her.

You can sometimes go sooner, although 30 minutes is about the soonest you wish to do this. You're getting right into the awkward region ... so break the ice before, then if you wait a lot longer than 3 or 4 hours and do not worry about getting a response; you're texting to start a conversation, not open a discussion. You'll still get dates and enthusiasts from ladies who do not respond to your icebreaker texts. It's merely crowning achievement if they do respond.

3: Don't Wait Too Long.

You know those old dating guides that tell you to wait for about three days or a week before calling a lady? Throw those manuals in the garbage bin; they'll do you no good.

When you meet her, run things based on exactly how your interaction went. Use these plans if she was excited about you when you met her, send her a text to set up the date the following day, or perhaps that day if you met her in the afternoon or morning. You'll discover you can fix dates for the list below or the same day with women that were delighted to meet you. These are always your best bet... the emotions are fresh, the desire is warm, and you produce that speedy love that most girls dream of experiencing all their lives.

If she was beautiful towards you when you met her, text her 1 or 2 days later. Indeed, 1 or 2 days should be enough time for her to "make up her mind," whether she intends to see you again ... however, not all the time, she'll have shed rate of interest altogether. If you wait.

Remember the maxim on here: move faster. If you wait too long, some guy that knows this rule far better than you will beat you to the game. Or life may intervene with any number of other unexpected barriers.

Strike while the iron is hot, the orb on your own with an uneven blade (i.e., not such high chances to land her).

4: Don't Beat Around the Bush

If you lurk about and try to deceive girls into liking you and dating you, girls will respond subsequently and also slip around to try to trick you right into being platonic friends with them.

That's why all the "text her until she's ready for a date" techniques don't work that well. You cannot test your way into someone's heart.

You've to do that personally. If you're sending messages that do n't suggest a meet-up in the original text (in addition to an icebreaker text), you are eluding. Why? Because she knows you want something, but you aren't saying what it is.

Nothing concealed. No beating around the bush. Just some light pleasantries, and then you define what you want clear as day.

It's brief and straight to the point-- and also does not make her wonder at all what you're after. Females react better and even much more consistently to this than any kind of another texting style you'll ever before use (" respond" here suggests establishing a date with you, instead of becoming part of an engaging but ultimate productive text banter/conversation, which appears to be most men's concept of a woman being "responsive").

5: Keep Texts Short

Your very first message to kick off a new discussion can be a little bit of an exemption to this ... so that you have enough space to fit the pleasantries in preparation for the ask. Aside from that, your texts ought to not be much longer than the last you got from her.

That means if she sends you a text as follows:

Her: Hey Fred, didn't speak with you recently: What's up?

Don't send her:

You: Hey Jane, sorry I didn't respond faster! I was, in fact, very busy recently taking a trip to meet some new customers. It's truly amazing stuff but a lot of work. When I was in Vegas, though ... Wait up until you hear that one. I got to see the Cirque du Soleil! Anyway, what've you been up to? I hope all's been well. We still on for lunch this Thursday?

That's alright, and it's great stuff, but it's way too much as a reply to a brief text. If you've been excellent with her, she'll simply view it as you being passionate regarding a remarkable week. She'll see it as you attempting to force a connection if you haven't.

Rather, send her this:

You: Sorry Jane, I relied on my eyeballs recently: Tell you about it when I see you. Still lunch on Thursday, yes?

On the other hand, if a woman sends you a wall surface of the message, don't send her "Cool" or "Let's do it" as feedback. She'll feel uncomfortable and as though you aren't as curious about her as she is in you.

You want her to feel your passion level very closely match hers. To do that, you'll want to keep your text brief-- and comparable in length.

6: Ask and Share Something Personal to Relate

Imagine last week you met someone at a networking conference. Merely a healthy individual.

Then imagine it's a couple of days later on, and you've mostly forgotten about this individual. Now, he sends you a text. Which of these three is the most likely to get a "yes" response out of you?

Text A:

Acquaintance: Tim, wish to order that beer we discussed tonight?

Text B:

Acquaintance: Hey, Tim, how would that outing go? Intend to grab that beer we talked about tonight?

Text C:

Acquaintance: Hey, Tim, just how would that outing go? I've got one of those myself showing up ... what a discomfort. Intend to order that beer we discussed tonight?

If you're like the majority of people, and your time is spiritual (if your time is more of a free-for-all, have a look at the 1922 article: "Why I Quit Being So Accommodating"), your reactions will be something like a lady's response to the same texts if they originated from a man she met a couple of days informally back. So now let's use your answers to the above messages and also leap into the mind of a woman and also see if you can now know with her:

Her response to Message A:

" Wait, who is this guy? Do I want to give him my evening?"

Certainly not a reaction you desire. Her response to Message B:

" Is this man attempting to butter me up since he desires something?"

Also, not a response you want. Her response to Message C:

" This person feels like not a bad guy. I can manage a fast drink."

Now you're on the best track. What's the distinction? Text C is an individual and relates to you.

There's a unique formula here: (a) welcome her with her name (yes, this is crucial, informal texters); then (b) ask her how something in her life went; next off, (c) associate with that, and share something similar from your life; and lastly, (d) ask her to meet you, with a refined reminder that she agreed to.

The name is to reinforce in her mind that this is a personal message and not a mass text message.

Asking her about something private is to get her to begin relating.

Sharing your own experience in the same vessel as the inquiry is to end up connecting by showing her that the two of you are not so different.

Asking her to meet you is getting to the point, and also staying (in passing! Don't put it out directly, unless you wish to maintain that you do not believe she's most likely to say yes). That she's said "yes" makes her remember why she said "yes" and makes her a whole lot more likely to say it once more this time around. Keep it personal.

#7:Avoid Asking Too Many Questions/Irrelevant Questions

This's simple. Don't walk around asking ladies weird/irrelevant, or even whole lots of questions through message. A straightforward, how would your X go?" is a rule that makes things much more personal. A question like "Shall we grab that coffee we talked about today?" is necessary, so a woman doesn't feel like you're unilaterally trying to decide for her. "Let's order that coffee we discussed today" is too enforcing and is likely to lead to resistance.

Both of these inquiries are great.

They're just two concerns: (1) an individual "procedure" type inquiry, and(2) a "get in" kind query regarding the day.

Aside from those 2, that's it. No other questions-- everything else is unimportant.

You'll talk with her, even more, when you see her face to face. No deep diving using text, my good friend; much of its effect is lost without the body language and nonverbal communication.

8: Ignore Unhelpful Questions and Topics

Often a girl may be on the fence about whether she wants you as a friend or a day. When this is the situation, she'll commonly attempt to wedge distracting or purposeless questions or topics into a text conversation. She does this to slow points down or steer you away from "date-like" tasks and towards "friend-like" ones.

That resembles this:

You: Haley, how was your weekend break? I hope you had a lot of rest. I was very careless all weekend break, but often you need weekend breaks like that. Hey, so how about we get hold of that bite we talked on today? Allow me to understand what your routine's appearing like, and let's get the gears working.

Her: Hey, Will ... omg, my weekend was crazy. Way too much alcohol consumption Saturday night, never doing that once again, lol! Lunch? Allow me to inspect what I have going on this week. Oh, btw, did you read about the new club they're opening up midtown next week? It's called "Motown." We should be most likely to that! I have a buddy that says he can get tickets.

They feel like something's incorrect right here ... this woman seems to be calling the shots. It doesn't feel entirely best saying, "Sure, let's go to that club opening ..." yet they do anyhow, because they do not think they have a choice.

They did not ignore purposeless things. They invited it to the front door and also left that door open for even more to maintain gathering instead.

Why's this negative? If it's not clear why letting women lead, most likely to have dates, and things of that nature are inferior for seduction,

Next, when you get hit with unhelpful and distracting subjects, simply duck and also weave:

You: Haley, how was your weekend break? I hope you got a great deal of rest. I was super lazy all through the weekend ... but occasionally you need weekend breaks like that. Hey, so how about we order that bite we discussed today? Let me know what your timetable's looking like and let's get moving.

Allow me to check what I have going on this week. Oh, by the way, did you hear about the new club they're opening up midtown following week? I have a buddy that says he can get tickets.

There is such a thing as too much clubbing, believe it or not ...

Well, check your schedule and let me know if the day's good for you on grabbing the bite. I've got Wednesday and Thursday free at lunchtime, and Saturday free right up till 8 o'clock - allow me to know if any would!

If the lady just wants you as a friend here, you'll receive an adverse feedback on the date. She'll be "busy" those times and also try to reschedule for a few other times. She does this to keep the advantage and stay in control-- which is what she requires to good friend-zone you.

However, if she's on the fence, she'll come back and eventually inform you one of those times is fine.

Be prepared to have to do a kick-ass works getting some sexual stress made up when you meet her. And have your sprezzatura at full blast. Have both of these in place, and also, you can run away that "feasible buddy" mantle she's curtained around your neck. Simply ensure you scoot!

9: Use Interesting Language

This set's more difficult to teach. It's best if you're well-informed and have a little experience writing. If you can pick fascinating, vibrant language out, it assists make your messages extra captivating.

A few vivid phrases to help you began:

" Shall we" as opposed to "Would you like to" or "Do you wish to" "Scoop you" rather of "Pick you up" (in an automobile, for a date, and so on) "Grab [lunch, a drink, etc.] or" Snag "instead of' Get" or" Have." Making use of verbs rather than nouns (e.g., "I napped" as opposed to "I took a nap").

Using active voice (" I got this" as opposed to "They gave me this").

Colorful language is simply more eye-catching, and also makes you more attractive, as well.

10: Vary Your Response Frequency.

When you're genuinely … when you're involved in a hundred things socially, this isn't a problem. Or you've got six different women you're seeing. Or you're running your very own organization. Or you've got a million tasks to handle for works. In these cases, your feedback time varies typically. It'll be lightning-quick often, and glacially slow others.

This is optimum. Women respond best to guys whose reaction time is unpredictable, yet within a specific range. Now, if you constantly take a day to react to her, or it occurs way too much, she'll likely auto-reject. Do not go crazy.

Permanently, don't also go extreme in either direction. If a lady regularly takes an hr to write you back, don't constantly write her back in 10 minutes. Instead, compose her again in 10 minutes one-time ... and 2 hours the following.

Action times will undoubtedly tend to vary usually for many active people. If you observe that a woman: (a) always texts you back after the very same quantity of time (e.g., 40 mins), or (b) always messages you again after the very same quantity of time that it took you to react to her last message, you know she's playing video games with you. Don't call her out on it, simply ... be conscious.

And play her game back much better than she recognizes exactly how-- vary your response times and don't be foreseeable.

You'll keep her guessing-- and fascinating.

11: Make Seeing You face to face the only Way to Talk with You

Like we said we read earlier in this book, women speak because they like to speak. And as you recall, we likewise discussed that ladies want men to "just be(platonic) friends" with.

How does that affect how you text ladies?

Simple: you do not offer them what they're searching for over text. A woman wants a texting buddy? Excellent!

That's not you.

A woman wants a person to go into an in-depth discussion with over SMS? Amazing!

It just isn't you.

She desires somebody to send her great deals of texts and also make her feel special? Impressive!

But she'll need to discover a person else for that.

The only point you utilize SMS message for is getting ladies out to meet you IN PERSON.

If she can get her fill of you using text, the probabilities of her coming out to meet you go down substantially reduced.

If she genuinely likes you … and if she truly wants to speak with you … and she can not get that from you via text message … and you will not speak to her on the phone much, either …

She WILL meet you.

And also, when both of you exist, in person and also in the flesh, you can work your magic.

12: Leave Something Small to Cover, and Send a Pre- Meeting Text

It's finest to leave some tiny information out that you can cover later when you set up the real logistics of a date. While this isn't entirely needed, it's handy for your pre-meeting text.

You almost always intend to use a pre-meeting text for two reasons. The first is you comfort your day that, of course, you remember the location and time, and you will certainly be there. This nixes any opportunity of her reneging of fear of you disappointing up. If she plans to flake, the second is that you provide her the opportunity to offer you a heads up. If she's going to be late or not make it at all, this makes certain you do not squander your time going someplace.

A pre-meeting text with a relevant detail you didn't discuss earlier will certainly appear like this:

You: Hey, Cassie! Heading out in 10 minutes; must be there right at 2 PM. I'll meet you at the subway terminal's South Exit.

A pre-meeting text if you do not have any particular relevant data to cover will appear like this:

You: Hey, Cassie! Heading out in 10 mins; ought to exist right at 2 PM. If I'm the first one there, I'll order a seat inside.

Either of these works simply fine and both comfort her you're going. Both also advise her to provide you a heads up if she isn't going, so you do not squander your time (and even get angry/annoyed).

Suppose she does flake; indeed, after that, stay tuned. We'll speak about merely what to do two phases from now.

Texting When It's Been a While

In some cases, you could have a situation where you shed touch with the woman for a while. Whether it's because it really did not go anywhere or you just failed to remember, you stopped texting her. And she stops texting you.

After that, one day, you come across her number once more or remember her, and you think, "Man, that girl was cute. I would certainly like to see her once again." However, it's been so long, and she's most likely gone on. How do you come back in touch?

The way you do this is with what I call the "check-in" message. It's a way to get with a girl you've lost touch with. And you do it in a nice, natural method.

The Standard Check-In Text

The conventional check-in text message consists of these five elements:

1. Welcoming and her name

2. Apologies for why you've been quiet

3. The explanation that you've been hectic

4. Ask her exactly how she is

5. Ask her out and request her schedule

The welcoming and name we've already covered in the chapter on just how to message a woman. So let's speak about the other 4.

The thing you "did wrong" makes you high status and also vital, yet her reduced status and unimportant. And now you desire to make it up to her. If you do, many of the women you message will certainly treat it like it is the situation.

You've been active: here, you just desire to claim you've been active. You can mention the "why" if you like, yet it isn't needed. You just intend to provide her an understandable reason for your absence. This makes your check-in text conforming ... you were active, and also now points have cleared (and also you have time for her). This is the "piece of new details" component of a brand-new text conversation.

Ask exactly how she is: as you recall, "consideration" is just one of 4 components to include in a new cold message. Here you ask exactly how she is to reveal consideration ... and likewise since it's just a regular point for people to do that have not talked in a while. In this manner, if she has anything essential she needs to upgrade you on, you've provided her a social home window to do so.

Ask her out and request her routine: and also last but not least, you wish to solve the reason: ask her for her timetable. In this manner, she doesn't have to question what the message has to do with it. She doesn't require to ask herself what you're after. It's right there in the message. "Oh, alright-- he intends to order beverages and also capture up."

Here's an instance of what these aspects appear like all placed with each other:

Hey Gina! Sorry I've been silent these past six weeks; I wasn't neglecting you, I simply got so pounded with my projects that whatever beyond works got pigeonholed up until life returned to peace of mind once again. Anyhow, things have cleared up a little bit. Exactly how you been? Allow me to understand your schedule over the following week or two, and also let's strategy to assemble and capture up on points.

Non-Standard Check-In Texts

The common check-in text will be your text reset support. It's what you'll use most of the moment, with many women. What do you do in more extreme scenarios? A participant of the Girls Chase online forums asks:

To steam it down to brass tacks, what's needed is a method to produce a rate of interest from a woman we have just me when, a year to 18 months ago, number close, great chemistry, however, no day or same evening lay. They could additionally still be simple & cost-free and also living close-by and would certainly benefit from costs time with us and our recently-realigned viewpoints on exactly how to offer her what she desires & needs through enjoyable & frolicsome experiences.

What do you do in these more severe scenarios ... where you barely know the lady, or it's been far also long considering that you talked to them? Well, you need something a bit more severe than the normal check-in text.

Choice # 1: Clearing Out My Phone

Your very first option is to go through your phone and also clear out old phone numbers that did not work out. As you erase old names, try to find women you 'd such as to take one more shot with. When you discover them, text them this:

I'm sorry I have not chatted with you in forever ... I just got caught up with things, and did not get in touch. Listen, I was going through erasing old numbers, and wanted to touch bases once more and also see what's up. Want to get a coffee at some point?

You'll get some amusing responses back to this. Some of these women will only very vaguely remember you (or they won't remember you at all) ... and they simply assume from the tone of the text that the two of you must have been close ... in some way.

They'll meet up with you, both unconvinced and intrigued, and also they'll wish to remember just how you satisfied. Typically you intend to be semi-vague below. Don't attempt to jog their memories entirely. The past isn't essential. Just treat them, like a good old friend, be sorry that you haven't complied with up, and get on with things.

You can get an incredible boost occasionally with these girls. They'll seem like because they've known you for so long, they do not have to be as on-guard with you as they are with most guys. And also you still get the benefit of getting on their romantic and also sex-related radar displays ... unlike the majority of the men, they've recognized a long period and have long because put right into the friend area.

You're the long-lost person they never got with, but that goes back into their lives. It's a beautiful place to be.

Choice # 2: Leaving Town

If you intend to leave the city (or country), you can select numbers out of your phone and text this:

I got caught up with some points before, and never finished up adhering to up with you way back when. I don't recognize what you're doing, however, if you 'd such as to order a warm chocolate or an ice cream before I'm out of below, I would certainly love to see you one last time ... Shall we do that?

In my experience, this message gets you a higher reaction rate than Option # 1 ... that is, she's extra likely to react. The price she comes out on a date is lower than with the initial option.

If you've got 10 or 20 numbers that never went anywhere and you're on your way out, there's no reason not to use it. You might surprise yourself with what you get from it.

Aren't These Texts Too Long?

The Law of Least Effort simply says one of the most socially powerful guy is the one who gets the best results for the least amount of initiative. If you can send one text, and also perform in one text what it takes most guys several texts and also hours of texting and waiting to do, that's lower initiative.

And when it's been a while, you require a long message like this to get your message through. If you think you're going to message her, "Hey Gina, what's going on? She doesn't remember you, or you have not talked with her, so you're unnecessary.

→ "Oh, I see, he was active. → "Oh, he wants to meet up with me. Busy individual has time for me now, huh?"

You wish to roll from one of those feelings to the following before they have time to cement. You do not desire the message to end with her reasoning, "Who is this man?" since when your following message comes, you're now an enigma. You don't want it to be upright, "Why is he texting me?" because now you need to combat her suspicion.

The long text with every little thing in it breaks social convention somewhat. Yet it's so exuberant therefore sincere that no matter. Ever get a thrilled, satisfied, yet likewise regretful long message from a girl? I have, lots of times, and you never care that it's long. You just catch the feelings she's sending over-- and those emotions feel excellent.

Example Text Conversation

While all this may seem made complex in the beginning glance, the tough work's all at the start. What excellent texting results in is vastly simpler message talks that line up days like dominos. All said and done, right here's an instant message conversation, start to end up, to provide you a feeling for what this appears like:

[an hour after meeting a new lady]

You: Happy to have made your acquaintance, buddy;-RRB- - [your name]

[two hours later on]

Her: Great to meet you as well!:-

[36 hours later on] You: Hey Sandy, how would the weekend break end up? I hope the rest of it was as remarkable as the starts were:-RRB- I wound up going to a pizza event with a number of people Sunday evening ... I haven't been to one of those given that I was 12. It was fun. And some wonderful pizza. On our bite today - when's helpful for you? My routine's rather open except Tuesday and Wednesday nights. Allow me to know what day's ideal, and we'll schedule it up.

[40 minutes later on]

Her: Hey! The pizza party appears fantastic! My weekend break was pretty cool ... Mostly simply recovering from Friday, lol. Just how's Thursday for meeting up? I'm complimentary most of the day.

[25 mins later]

Claim 1 o'clock in the afternoon? There's this impressive little café no one understands around on Green Avenue we can inspect out ... They have the most astonishing crepes around the globe.

[1 hour later on]

Her: That seems fantastic, let's do it! See you on Thursday!

[2 hours later]

You: Awesome - see you after that, Sandy!

[5 minutes later on]

Her: Hey, I'm running about 10 minutes behind. Sorry ...! I'm coming!

[3 minutes later on]

You: No, biggie. See you when you get right here!

Now compare that to the last ten texting conversations you had with females ... which are more challenging, and which are much less? The only challenging part here is in discovering the process. As soon as you've got it down, you can perform it flawlessly, successfully, and also continually ... and it's a point of pure elegance.

And also you'll rest there and take a look at the mobile phone of those poor ladies you're sleeping with or dating ... and you'll see the volumes and quantities of unaware dull concerns they get ... endless discussions they're mired in ... and really, incredibly witty and interesting messages they're inundated with ... and you'll drink your head at the individuals sending them.

" I used to be one of those people," you'll say to yourself. "But that ... was one more life.".

And after that thought will undoubtedly pass, and also you'll possibly never invest a 2nd idea on texting once more.

Where the Learning Curve Lies.

Most Significant Growth Areas for every Level.

Here are the most significant growth areas you can expect, depending upon where you're at with texting.

Development Areas for Beginner Texters.

As a novice, you'll wish to focus much of your interest in complying with locations:

Getting down timing. How quick or exactly how sluggish should you react? What days and at what times of day should you message? What type of message do you send out, and when?

Getting down structure. Your obstacle will certainly not merely be to get used to using the proper text structure, but to stick to it.

Anxiety overshooting. Eventually, you need to ask her out. Much better to find out to do it earlier.

Development Areas for Intermediate Texters.

One of the most critical locations to concentrate on as an intermediate texter is:.

Getting down concision. The more concise you can make your texts (while still packing in whatever you must pack in), the much better.

Fascinating without being the fool. You wish to consist of fun, humor, and interesting little bits in your texts. Nevertheless, you do not intend to be the clownish entertainer.

Just how you strike the best balance-- where you aren't dull, however also not over the top-- is just one of your essential difficulties at this stage.

Involving ladies properly. How do you get girls to, in fact, engage with you over text? Just how do you get them to take component? This is among your most prominent foci at this phase. As she takes part more, she does even more of the work to establish points up, and makes the courtship a lot more enjoyable for you.

Setting updates a lot more smoothly. Right here, you'll target elements like when and exactly how you schedule days, where you take women on dates, and just how you handle the ease of days. The far better you access this, the even more yeses you'll get, and also the fewer flakes you'll see.

Growth Areas for Advanced Texters.

The primary targets for the sophisticated texter to boost upon are:.

Reducing texting a lot more. What's the bare minimum of messages you need to send before you can get a lady on a date? The closer to this you get, the much less possibility you offer yourself to mess things up, and also the earlier you'll get her out.

Getting women to chase you and also seek you. Wouldn't it be wonderful if women worked to establish dates themselves? This is something you'll find yourself having fun with more at this phase (and starting to be successful at).

Getting very dominant and straight, both in exactly how you established your dates, and in how you deal with the more exceptional reasons of language framework in texts. The objective is to be powerfully dominant without being imperious. Attractive, instead than undesirable.

CHAPTER FOUR

What to do When She doesn't Text Back

Things That Lead to Unreturned Texts and also Calls

Think of a woman you that you such as, who you invested maybe 30 or 40 minutes talking to in your initial experience. She was captivating, attractive, precisely your kind.

Got her in your head?

Now, if you can, remember how you felt the initial time you called her or texted her. I nearly didn't call a girl who was to become my sweetheart for two years. It was just as well frightening to dial her number on the phone.

Guess what? Yep: that occurs to girls, also.

Now, it isn't always the reason. In reality, it's just one of four primary reasons we'll talk about that may trigger her to not respond to you. Yet nervousness and also pressure is one of the Big 4 Reasons why ladies may not meet.

This set's most likely the most unusual reason for a great deal of men, to make sure that's why I chose to lead with it. But there are three various other reasons, as well. The four reasons ladies may not respond to you are:

Also much anticipation/nervousness: if a girl likes you a whole lot, she can be "too reluctant to reply." She can place a lot of pressure on herself to do well with you ... or be too anxious to type out a reply or address your telephone call. She may want to speak with you, yet never finish up doing so.

Too much of a state-shift: this one's a little harder to get your mind around at first, so I'll utilize an instance. Claim you met an excited girl at an event, hit it off, and took her phone number. She will look at your message and think to herself, "I cannot talk to him right now; it's too many words ..." and after that just never get back to you.

She wasn't all that interested: this sometimes occurs to every person. Stand up to the lure to connect every no-response to disinterest. This is what many people do (" I guess she didn't like me besides"). It's quite often one of the various other three reasons that's to criticize. Occasionally it is just that she had not been as interested as she appeared. It takes place.

Of these four reasons, # 3 and # 4 are the most convenient to fix.

Number 3 (poor closings) you repair when you get your closing structured. Make use of these suggestions and get even more technique choosing closes, and you'll begin to self-correct and get smoother and even more natural with time.

Number 4 (she simply isn't interested) you repair as you come to be more in harmony with

the signals females are providing you You expend more familiar with just how to inform a woman wants you. Then, you plain and straightforward don't take call details from girls you know aren't that interested.

Because they like you,) is harder to correct, number 1 (women who're as well nervous to react. You need to minimize uneasiness and make the most of comfort while you're there in person with her ... plus, you've got to make sure that the call you have with her later is hot and friendly. She has to feel comfortable reacting to you, above all.

Number 2 (ladies that have a large mood shift in between the time you meet and the time you message) is the hardest to deal with. The objective is that when such a lady gets your text or phone call later, when they're in a much less spicy mood, it won't also feel tough for her to respond.

These four adjustments might need you to upgrade you entirely.

Communications with girls ... specifically, if you're an energetic, high-energy individual.

Fortunately, however, exists's a faster way around all these discovering contours. That shortcut is ...

Spend Less Time with Girls and Get Them RespondingMore

Less time invested with a girl before you go for her call details does something unique for you. First, it allows you to evaluate out girls that aren't a lot right into you. It additionally lets you cut out the negative stuff: women that get so into you they're too terrified to speak to you later on; girls who get used to talking to you in a too- various power degree from their current power level; and bad closings to your communications with women.

Said another method, less time upfront has to do with as close to a magic bullet for the"women not texting back" trouble as you can get.

The ladies that are right into you right off the bat aren't time wasters. They may well take pleasure in the long conversation they have with you ... or perhaps they're simply attempting to be polite with someone that took the time to method and talk to them.

A woman's smiles, giggles, and talks with you are reactions. Her relocating someplace with you, or providing you her number when you ask for it quick ... those are a couple of examples of results. Outcomes are what you need, no matter how promising (or otherwise) your reactions might be.

You get an actual result when you ask for the number quickly. The ladies that like you will gladly give their own. The ones who aren't so inclined will wait, or refuse outright.

Expeditious means to sift the wheat from the chaff.

When a Girl Doesn't Text Back

You met a woman, ended up with her number, today you've called or texted her and she hasn't responded. What to do?

When a girl doesn't message back, or when a woman does not call back ... first, do not panic. It's not the end of the world. It doesn't imply you've lost her completely.

It just implies she hasn't returned to you yet.

Determination. It's the difference between the guys that want it and get it, and

the guys who do not. There were people I mentored who would have women disappear and act indifferent, but they would certainly just continue. Eventually, the ladies would certainly re-emerge, agree to meet, and also ultimately wind up in bed.

Persistence via text or phone can work wonders ... But it's essential to linger in a cool, laid back, socially savvy way. Do not get mad at ladies for not responding.

Instead, here are some things to bear in mind ... so you continue in the type of intelligent, appealing means probably to make a lady wish to chat to you once again:

Don't get accusatory or mad. Yes, it may appear impolite that she hasn't responded yet ... you're an unfamiliar person! She does not understand you from Jack again, and also doesn't understand what a remarkable guy you are. Angering is 100% guaranteed to scare her off. Abstain from anything like, "I don't understand why you're so aloof."

Do not get whiny. Simply as poor as mad is sad: whiny, complain-y males are a.

Huge turnoff to every girl out there. You would not care to get something like that from a woman ... and also a girl will care even much less to get something like that from a man.

Do be nonchalant. "Hey Karen, figured I 'd drop you a line since we have not attached in a couple of weeks. I just returned from the East Coast and the beginning.

- Chase" Treat the circumstance as if no one is to blame, and also the 2 of you are just reconnecting after a little time off, merely busy with your points. Calls and texts are not the area to air grievances or bandy about poor emotions. That's the kind of point that makes a lady desire to select up the phone and talk to you ... because she likely does not get it anywhere else in her life.

DO refrain from being also entertaining. "Just saw the most impressive motion picture today!" "OMG, assume my head is going to take off, you'll never think what just took place to me ...!!!" Anything like that is no good. That sort of stuff is perhaps alright three or four messages right into a conversation with a lady. To send that as a cold message, as your text opener, drips of try-hard reaction-seeking. Worse, in my experience, it rarely works. And also, when it does work, it gets you to focus from curious girls, not interested ladies. Stick to regular stuff, and you'll do great.

Don't be worried about providing a girl a little time off if she doesn't respond for a while. My regulation of thumb is something like this: she doesn't reply when: provide her a day of radio silence. She doesn't respond twice in a row: provide her 2 - 3 days of radio silence. She doesn't respond three times in a row: offer her a week of radio silence.

If she's still silent, you might try something bolder, depending on the scenario. There's no unique, proven method to reengage a girl who isn't reacting. It's most likely to vary by the reason that she does not respond, to begin with.

If she's as well timid, a beautiful, cozy voicemail could work ... or reduce.

Your messages if you've come across regarding entertaining, gamey, or insincere.

On the other hand, if it seems like excessive of a state-shift for her, share some more normal information of your life and inquire about hers. Often that's all it requires to assist her in seeing you as more "human" ... and also get her to respond.

When Texts Don't Work, Use Phone Calls

In some cases, You've Got to Change the Medium.

I wish to discuss a fun little method. This tech helps you get in touch with a way to get somewhere with women that don't react well.

This method is, simply, changing backward and forward in between texting and also calling.

Now, if you've done things right from the beginning with a lady, you won't usually require to utilize this. A great impression, mounting for the day before you get the number, after that strong message video game to establish points up ... that's generally most likely to do whatever you require it to do.

Generally, if you need this method, it's since you've done glitch: you made a weak very first perception, you didn't make it clear you desired a date with her, or it can be your texting was weak.

She has just established a bad criterion and secured negative feelings to messages from you. Sometimes a girl might get it in her head that "XYZ point is difficult" (like when you fit on her routine) for reasons she isn't aware of (anchoring).

For any type of such a scenario, you have one neat device in your toolbox: just vary the means of correspondence. In this phase, I'll show you how to do that by switching between texts and also phone telephone calls.

Objections to Text/Call Splitting.

There are three main arguments to text/call splitting, so let's address those.

1. If she does not react to my messages, why trouble?

2. Isn't making a call intrusive?

3. Isn't using telephone call dated/outmoded in today's day and age?

1: Why Bother?

This objection is no different from anything else with conference ladies: "Cold approach is hard. Why bother?" "Men need to lead. Why can't I await ladies to lead?" "All this 'find out game' stuff is a great deal of work. Why not just be myself instead?" The solution here is the same: because it works.

Not everyone intends to do every little thing, which I comprehend. Yet if you're an individual who won't use text/call split because he does not wish to, after that whines that females do not text him back ... well, that's simply foolish.

Some individuals view such strategies (where you remain to comply with up with a lady that isn't bursting at the joints for you) as the chase. Sure, they are ... if you're doing them incorrectly; however, you can say that of anything.

Picture this: an active, important male satisfies a gorgeous woman. He messages her to meet up several times, yet it does not turn out. Meanwhile, he's taking place dates with various other girls, also.

One day on his way to the gym, he gets his phone and calls this woman. She answers, they chat, he establishes a day with her before the telephone call ends, and also after that, he hangs up and goes on about his day.

Chasing? No.

This is how you'll be using this strategy.

2: Isn't Making a Phone Call Intrusive?

Not as invasive as what you'll be doing to her in the bedroom.

To a certain level, you wish to be considerate of a girl's time and not place way too much stress on her beforehand (before you're fans). A minimum of this is precisely how you wish to kick points off. I'll inform you of a secret, though ... not all females are produced equal.

Some ladies desire a guy that'll leave a minimal footprint on their lives-- one that'll make things simple and low pressure for them, and take up little of their time. Other ladies desire a male who's most likely to impose himself on them in smart and eye-catching means. They prefer a man that will certainly require them to take note of him.

The wonderful feature of the text/call split technique is that it begins out: "I'll be awesome, and also we'll do this in an unimposing way." If she does not respond to that method, it switches over to: "Hey, I'm vital, so let's set this up.".

Dating itself is an invasive process. You intrude on her time, invade her thoughts and desires, and finally horn in her body. If you're (excessively-- a little is great) stressed regarding being "also intrusive" with a woman you intend to copulate with ... well, possibly it's time for a little asshole training.

Additionally, remember, some girls like telephone calls over message. By beginning with the message, then moving to the phone if it isn't working, you enable yourself to cover both groups.

3: Aren't Phone Calls So 20th Century?

There's additionally this objection that asks: "Who makes a phone call anymore?" The answer, of course, is "active individuals." Call just is just the most beautiful interaction medium for a particular sort of talk.

When you try to set something up over message, and it isn't working, the just.

Individuals that maintain texting are trainees with excessive time on their hands and other individuals that don't have a lot of things to do.

That does not indicate YOU have to just text ladies in university or ladies with also much time on their hands. They recognize and appreciate an excellent phone telephone call from a hectic male as a lot as anyone else.

The hectic person simply calls. As opposed to 100 text and half a day of inputting and also waiting, he can complete everything with a 2-minute phone telephone call.

You will be active if you are successful with females. And the type of male women find appealing are those who are busy. Among things you'll discover is that the busier you get, the much easier dating gets, and it's not a coincidence. Busyness works as a sort of implicit preselection. If it's evident, you do not have a big amount of time for her (without you being "fake hectic"), that states advantages regarding you. It states you reside in abundance and have points that are very important to you in your life.

Another option to the text/call split is the "round in your court" message (we'll speak about it in two phases). You can utilize one of these methods, or both of them. If you've now done a few phone telephone calls, and she still will not come out, you will want to do a "ball in your court phone call" call rather than text ... yet we'll chat regarding that later on.

Another group of individuals that choose calls to messages are lonely individuals. You'll locate some girls might be slow to respond or non- receptive over text, however really receptive over the phone-- particularly if they are sad, lonely, or depressed. Phone is simply an extra individual tool, and one that's much better for individuals who prefer a more personal touch.

Phone calls are as great now as they always have been IF your phone video game is good (same IF as it's constantly been). Like anything, this is a skill you have to educate, and it takes a little time. If you aren't used to chatting on the phone, it can feel like phone calls aren't working that fantastic for you, because they aren't yet.

Ways to Call/Text Split.

These days, I suggest you typically start with texts. But not constantly. We'll cover scenarios where you desire to lead with a telephone call a little later in this phase. Normally, you will lead with texting. That's because it's simple, low stress, and the learning curve's much shorter than call.

You only require to be great at standard logistics-handling messages to get dates with a text video game, supplied naturally; you're doing whatever else right before you get the contact number. So it minimizes the level of skill you require to get dates, which is what long-distance document is everything about: get her out in individual with you.

You need to type only utilize telephone call nowadays when one or even more of the following holds: (a) you sent her icebreaker and follow-up texts, and she did not respond; (b) you tried to establish a day(s) through message, and she flaked or didn't meet; (c) she has continuously dodged day demands or is challenging to select.

In each of these cases, the phone telephone call ups the ante. Continuing to text when she's incredibly elusive placements you as the chaser. She may call back; she may not.

My general referral on when to use text/call splits vs. the ball-in- your-court message is: if you're "meh" regarding the woman, toss the sphere in her court; if you 'd like to see the girl, text/call split. You'll often tend to discover phone calls have a far better percent than ball-in-her-court texts if you're excellent at phone video games. Phone calls are additionally a heck of a whole lot more time effective.

That indicates, if you don't have a great deal of time (say, you'll leave community soon), OR you simply wish to get this girl ASAP (if she'll be off the market soon ... or if you just really like her), there's no point claiming you do not care-- and jumping her the "it's in your court" text-- when you do care. You also do not need to wait two weeks for her to decide she desires to date you, either.

If you want her-- and texts aren't working-- after that call her. Right here's how you do that in 4 steps.

Action # 1: Good Text/Impression Game.

How likely she is to answer your phone call is straight tied to exactly how reliable your text message game is, and just how excellent a very first impression you made. If your text video game was unique and also your first impression was good, she's going to tend to desire to answer your telephone call.

Women are regularly looking for good emotions. They will invite you into their lives if they watch you as somebody who can provide these. That means: do not simply slouch with your messages and think you'll call her if it does not exercise. You still require a good message game. Without that, she's less most likely to answer your call.

Action # 2: Time It Properly

Particularly if you're new, it's essential to provide her enough time to react to messages.

Some ladies take hours to get back to you; some can take a day. This does not always suggest they aren't interested; although, if she does not respond in 3 or 4 hours, you possibly have work to do as soon as she's on the date. It can merely suggest a girl's busy, or keeps her phone on silent, or doesn't check messages a lot. Believe it or not, there are ladies around that don't check their messages often ... mainly professional ladies or others with a lot going on.

So do not fall into the catch where you text a woman, she doesn't respond right

away, and afterward, 90 minutes later, you're calling her. It looks clingy and also frightened, as you rested around looking at your phone, and even called when you did not listen to back.

Instead, a joint development could look something like this:

1. Meet the lady

2. [3 hrs later] Ice-breaker message

3. Follow-up plus date-ask

4. Phone call with date-ask

5. [IF no date/ evades-- 3 days later on] Text invite to something different

6. [, if no date/ evades-- 2 days later] Bonding call without any date-ask

7. [3 days later] Phone call with date-ask

8. [IF says no/ evades-- 3 days later on] Text welcome to something various

9. [IF states no/ dodges-- that evening] Ball-in-your-court phone call

That's five days invite in two weeks without feeling rushed, packed- in, or try-hard. That's respectable. It's great because it filters for as lots of variables as feasible: perhaps she doesn't desire a day eventually you ask; however she does on an additional; possibly she does not like among your date suggestions, so you cycle via others; maybe she does not like one medium (messages), yet enjoys to get a call.

You provide in your room to find an angle that works for a lady where previous perspectives did not make when you switch over tactics up.

Action # 3: Keep It Fresh

You want to talk about some topics you've previously covered ... while at the same time presenting new details, ideas, and stimulations. Do not be the man who invites her to coffee on Monday, gets a "Not right now, thanks," after that messages her again welcoming her to coffee on Thursday ... after that messages her once again on Sunday to welcome her to coffee once again.

Rather, be the individual who welcomes her to coffee on Monday, then welcomes her to an art gallery opening on Thursday. That's for two reasons: it provides you the opportunity to strike on something she'll claim "yes" to, and it makes you much more fascinating: "What's Scott going to recommend this time?"

For the call, comply with the call overview and also make certain you have a.

The current narrative prepped to go. You will not always need it, yet it's convenient to have resting there at-the-ready. You can introduce right into your tale to warm up the discussion up if she does not delve into the conversation right away.

Action # 4: Texts for Logistics, Phone Calls for Bonding.

Maintain this regulation in mind: the text is for logistics, phone telephone calls are for bonding.

If you had a fast communication when you initially met her (e.g., a 2-minute number close) ... or you didn't have the best communication. After that kind of stumbled the follow-up over text ... you might require to do a little bonding before she feels comfortable enough to meet you. That's where the call can be found in.

Don't use texts to attempt to build connections, as a result of the lack of context. You can joke about messages, and you can set up logistics, but they aren't excellent for much else. Your sexy bedroom voice plus 10 mins speaking to her on the phone can be enough to swing a great deal of ladies from "on the fencing about you" to "completely on board.".

The greater context of call likewise makes them extra immune to negative anchoring. If she begins connecting negative emotions with your texts (" He's too aggressive" or "His texts are boring" or "He always messages me at bothersome times"), it's easy for her to secure these emotions to you and not desire to respond to. However, with a telephone call, specifically, if you're proficient at phone video games, it's straightforward to infuse interest, selection, and power. These make it simpler for you to anchor stable positive emotions ... insomuch that even if she declines a few days, or if you don't always call at convenient times, you still provide energy that makes her intend to answer your call.

If she appears unclear regarding you over text, or she's dodgy, call her. It ups the stake (" Okay, let's get major about this") and reassures (and re-attracts) her in means texts can not.

Call/Text Splitting Caveats.

There are some caveats to what we've laid out in this short article, also. These are that you have to call FIRST if you're time-pressed or if she's clearly warm for you and that when you've introduced calling, any type of ball-in-your-court interaction has to more than a call, not text. Below's what these two caveats mean.

When to Call First.

The regular policy is: lead with texts, comply with (if needed) with a telephone call. Often you don't have time for texting and also waiting, waiting, and texting.

When you're simply around for a few days, for instance, texting can murder your odds to see a lady once again. Even if she intends to meet you, by the time you get it all arranged, you may already be on your train or trip out of there.

In this situation, also, if leading with a phone call possibly isn't the social standard in itself, still do it. If your phone game is good, it won't matter, because as soon as she's on the phone, she'll be enjoyed to talk with you again.

Also, in some cases, you meet a lady, and you can inform she's very thrilled to meet up with you once again. When this holds, it's commonly better to lead with telephone calls over texts.

Leading with calls brings her back to a more productive interaction channel, which is what she wants. Ideally, she intends to be with you, not be talking with you at a distance. Telephone calls are a lot closer to really being with you than messages are. You can call, advise her what she's so ecstatic regarding, and get her to meet up, with any luck pronto.

You might face the scenario where a lady is piping hot for you in-person, then you start to massage her, and she grows cool. And also after that you call her once again, and she's warm again. What's taking place below is the texting is a disappointment for her. She does not desire to connect with words on a screen that represents you. She wishes to connect with you. When you have ladies that like you, you might find you're much better off with phone calls instead of texts.

What happens if the initial telephone call doesn't get you a day? No worry; just usage.

Text/call splitting, and remain to switch it up.

What Medium to Use with Ball-in-Her-Court Messages.

Usually, the ball-in-her-court message is done using a message. Nonetheless, if you present a call, you need to do this via phone, not message. The reason why is because phone telephone calls are a more severe, a lot more "genuine" tool than text.

If you're now talking to her using telephone call and you provide her an incredibly "real" message like "When you've got time and intend to grab a beverage, drop me a line and let me understand" over text, it comes throughout as a little afraid. Oh, so he can speak with me over the phone about ABC and also DEF; however, he can't tell me I'm preventing him and ask me to allow him to know when I'm prepared over the phone? Scaredy feline!

Do not ask her out and additionally offer her a ball-in-her-court message in the very same phone call; it appears spiteful. Do not do this:

You: ... blah blah. Anyhow, we should order one of those mojitos you keep chatting about-- want to do that this week?

Her: You know, today's active for me. I do not assume I can.

You: Okay. Well, it appears like you're always pretty active lately. Inform you what; I'm not so efficient the entire chasing-you-around point, so why don't we leave it off for some time, and then when you've got a long time, you can drop me a line and let me know when you intend to assemble?

Feels like you're sort of whiney or bitter right here, does not it? That's since you're instantly complying with the rejection up with the ball-in-your-court message. This is various in text. Since a text message is much less individual, whatever feels much less severe. Her decreasing your day isn't that big of a deal, simply like you tossing the ball in her court isn't one either. So you can follow up a turned down day request with a ball-in-her-court message. It does not seem like you're stating this just because your feelings are harmed.

However, for the call ball-in-her-court, you require to make points differently. Rather, ask her out utilizing text, and if she dodges/rejects, call her that night and have a short (2 or 3 min) phone call ... then ball-in-her-court her.

That resembles this:.

[2 to 3 mins of tiny talk/chit-chat]

You: Yeah, so anyway, it looks like you're incredibly busy/tough to meet!

Her: Yeah, you know, I work lengthy hrs, and this work I'm on today is drawing up all my downtime.

You: I entirely understand. I had a project like that about four months ago. It was fun, yet my social life just vanished. Hey, so, I don't intend to keep calling you and texting you and distracting you when you're so active, and I'm also dreadful at the entire chasing thing, as you can most likely inform. [pause; allow her to laugh] So I'll quit bugging you for now; however, I 'd like to meet up with you at some time and stop being unfamiliar people over a phone line. Inform you what, when you get some spare time, fire me a message or give me a telephone call and let's assemble, that work?

Say your farewells and get off the phone.

Keep in mind the distinction in tone and also message structure from the ball-in-your-court text message. It's a lot more conversational here, and you put more time in to communicate, "I get where you're originating from, and I comprehend." That's since the phone is a richer tool, and also, you must make it clear you're not saying this because you're starting.

The reason you call her that night steams down to a fundamental property of operant conditioning. That is, favorable punishment (eliminating something she enjoys) works finest when it closely follows the negative behavior it penalizes.

In this case, her cleaning apart yet one more day request is the bad behavior. The decisive penalty is that now you're going to wait for her to call you. And also, you aren't going to call her and provide good feelings, happiness, and enjoyment any more.

If you do this 2 or 3 days after being rejected, or even the next day, the sensation has waned, and also, she won't link the penalty to the habits. That makes her less likely to assume "Oops-- I created this; I did glitch ... I would certainly better fix it if I desire the fellow feelings back." Rather, she's more most likely to believe, "Hmm, I presume he's simply offering up," or "Maybe he found somebody else; I need to carry on, as well possibly.".

If you need to use the ball-in-your-court telephone call, time is essential.

CHAPTER FIVE

Myths about Women

There is much disinformation in our society relating to dating. That's why it's essential to utilize your mind and to trust your intestine.

While the full description about various myths would undoubtedly be the subject of a whole different other books, I would certainly still such as to briefly clear up why the individuality qualities and activity reasons referenced over tend to lead to successful dating.

Females have standard needs-- simply like guys. Nonetheless, they are different from male needs. Culture also places a lot of limits and stress on ladies, and males need to recognize that.

Females are not seeking males that play games and are usually uninterested in playing games themselves, despite what prominent society would certainly have you believe.

As women and men, both advance, communication, and also partnerships will become increasingly more healthy and balanced and also meeting. That's why you might require to throw away several of the preconceived notions regarding ladies that you've been force-fed all your life by family, buddies, associates, or TV.

That's why it's so crucial for you to be helpful and charitable for your girl. It's a whole great deal more challenging for women than for men to advance financially. That claimed, it does not suggest that you require to end up being a doormat for a lady that does not care to do anything in her life.

Even successful women require a man! This indicates that you still need to embrace some of the traditional works while being open-minded and encouraging to the woman's life, her objectives, and her challenges. Yes, this implies a little bit more work, but it features better advantages.

While a few of your pals might claim that you need to concentrate on amount instead of quality, in the long-lasting, it's a losing recommendation. Why? Since while others develop and expand in partnerships, consequently brightening their skills for future encounters, you'll be left behind.

Experience and technique are vital. You need to see what helps you and what does not. This is what will make you a hero over time.

While being a gamer sounds attractive to numerous guys, usually, they recognize that there is no actual compound to it-- on their own or for the females. It's a lot easier to claim what your goals and objectives are in advance and also to have a true partnership. It will be a great deal for both.

The 5 Most Damaging Mistakes About Texting a Girl

Texting ahead of time

This looks like a no brainer, but it is a refined point. Discharging off a message right after meeting a person, typically is not a good concept. Also, if they are throughout you, you still show some restraint. Waiting a day or 2 to get in touch with for the very first time shows emotional maturation and power. Leaving the texting conversation initially or not texting as usual as she interacts that you remain in need. Something as simple as this often plants a seed of uncertainty, which will undoubtedly draw her as well you like iron to a magnet.

Being sexual

Texting too often, as well as quickly is the most typical texting mistake, yet being excessively sexual is the most damaging when texting ladies. What a lot of people do not get is that ladies have an integrated hereditary concern of guys that can be caused by a sneeze.

If you have not created sufficient convenience in the connection, sending out even the slightest sex-related message will trigger her "RUN AWAY!" impulse. She will undoubtedly perceive that the sexual is your only passion, and if you are creepy in the slightest, it's around.

To double up on this concern, no woman, also the most promiscuous lady (think me I have evaluated this), refuses to be regarded only for sex. It may be 100% real that she wishes to breach you to the same degree, yet you can not be the one open this door. When discovering exactly how to text a woman, make her feel secure first, and also, I assure you if there is attraction, sexual intimacy will adhere to.

Being overly aggressive/cocky

There is a big distinction between being cocky/funny and just being a jerk. He got on a high from his previous success, yet he took it too far with this lady.

The trouble is when you run into a lady who can't hang with this or just is unaware as to just how to react. If you are playing tennis with a 5-year-old, lob the damn round, do not send it flying at their face.

It is also lovely/boring.

I see this at all times when I show people exactly how to message girls. They do not recognize just how to message a girl in a means that produces stress, develops tourist attraction. Playing it risk-free is very easy; however, it gives the least return on your efforts. In various other words, if you gamble at nickel ports, you will never get the big payout.

Him: Hey, wow, it was wonderful to meet you last evening.

Her: Yeah, you appear lovely.

Him: I am, yet you are not just sweet, however, so cute!

Her: Wow, you are not so bad on your own (She is flattered, however gently repulsed).

Him: So cutie, what are you doing tomorrow, love to get you dinner.

Her: Thanks a lot but I need to ... (Laundry my hair, wax my base, etc.).

It isn't because ladies like jerks a lot more, yet it is because the shake develops stress and that stress is sexy. I know you have experienced the same point with that truly wonderful, actually charming lady you discarded. When texting ladies, you should push the limits, you must be fascinating, or you will certainly never be sufficient.

Connection warnings.

This is more of a girl point to draw, but I have gotten plenty of e-mails from men who have broken this. Here are instances of offensive partnership ultimatum messages:.

Hey, I genuinely like you, and I would love to understand where this is going?

If I text you, I would genuinely, such as a message back faster, seem like you do not care.

I feel like I am the just one working on this relationship.

I am not cool down with you having so many person pals.

I truly like you, and I don't want to play any kind of more games.

All of these texts are interacting, "I am weak, I require reassurance that you care, you have even more power than me, I am envious, and also I am imitating a woman." , if you write this kind of text, you require her right into an extra male duty. She will act appropriately and run away, just like you would. Allow her to relocate in the direction of you initially, then inform her you feel the same. Always keep the equilibrium when texting women, continually be the one in control of your emotions.

Also though many guys assume they understand just how to text women to build attraction and rate of interest, many of them regularly dedicate basic errors that finish up murdering any type of attracting the lady might have had.

The awful part is, these are easy errors that could easily be stayed clear of. There are three very typical yet extremely deadly blunders that people often make.

I'm most likely to inform you what they are and, likewise, just how to fix them. See if you are guilty of a few of these mistakes and make sure to do them once again exceedingly.

OK, below we go ...

Harmful Text Game Error # 1: NOT Waiting Until You Get A Reply Before Sending Her Even More Messages.

You need to never send out a girl several text without her very first reply back to your original message. The only exemption is when your first message did not get provided, and also your phone offers you a mistake message.

Various other than that, you ought to always wait up until she reacts to your very first text before you pound her inbox with even more messages.

Why, you ask?

Because refraining from doing so only interact with her that you are hopeless and clingy. Similar to a lot of the lovable losers that she 'd engaged with in the past.

This is a substantial turn off for women!

It decreases your worth and gives her power over you. The more you maintain texting her without her replying, the much more it emerges that she is the prize, and you are merely asking to talk to her.

Just keep in mind, you merely me this woman. Don't offer her the impression that you are now selecting the wedding celebration dress.

Harmful Text Game Error # 2: Making Your First Text To Her Boring.

The very first text message to a woman you simply me is one of the most crucial texts you will certainly ever send her. This is the text that will mainly determine whether she react back to you, so don't make it uninteresting!

Most people make the first message they send resemble this:.

" Hi, this is John from the club last evening. I just intended to claim Hi, which I truly appreciate meeting you ... blah blah.".

Don't do that! It's monotonous and also, even worse, it doesn't oblige her to respond.

Right here is an unfortunate fact that you need to understand ...

You Are Not Special To Her!

OK, perhaps I didn't need to shriek. Sorry regarding that.

However, pay attention, the fact is, the lady (especially if she's hot) most likely offered her numbers bent on several different men last evening (women do that.) Sending some vanilla text messages is not going to make her remember you. And also, if she does not recognize you, she won't respond!

Rather you should say something attention-grabbing that additionally associates with the time when you satisfied her. Something like ...

" Man, what was the deal with that insane guy on the dancing floor last night?! I think he gave me a shiner - John".

Or ...

" Oh my god. I simply realized who you resemble ...".

Ladies are VERY interested in their looks, and also this declaration is sure to pique her passion.

By bring up something amusing or intriguing that happened last night, you not just remind her that you yet likewise draw her back to the psychological state that she was in when she satisfied you (and having fun.) This is a very powerful strategy and also extremely important for building tourist attractions (a lot more on this in various other articles.).

Harmful Text Game Error # 3: Sending Texts That Are Too formal.

Remember, you are trying to talk to this woman, not audit her tax obligations. So do not send her messages like ...

" Dear Stacey, I'm pleased we had an opportunity to speak last evening, and I had a delightful timc ...".

Instead, speak with her like you 2 are already friends. Be playful, teasing, and enjoyable. Don't be afraid to use jargon, misspellings, and unfinished sentences. If she is foreign or is highly informed and is turned by bad grammar and slang.), (The obvious exception would certainly be.

Male, I think I simply had the weirdest day of my life. Yours has to be quite insane, I wager.".

This message likewise offer to excite her inquisitiveness and make her wonder what was so strange about your day.

Remember, our supreme goal is to escalate the messages to this woman to a sex-related degree, so it's best to begin off with a lively tone instead of an official one.

Now you may be thinking that you'd never make these stupid errors, but I can not inform you the number of men I've seen repetitively make these text mistakes and destroy their chances to sleep with so many hot girls.

Don't make the same errors. The challenges that I've discussed could seem necessary but by avoiding them, you can increase or triple your chances with a girl.

Texting Women - What You Don't Know Can Hurt You

Hundreds and hundreds of ladies from throughout the globe have the same view when it comes to guys and their texting methods, they are clueless. We rant and also rave when one gets it right. If we have relocated onto another, we conserve their messages and carry them around on our phones too.

Guys, when texting, women are just doing communications at a minimum. They aren't engaging the female or her spirited nature. If you are sending anything similar to the following as texts, you may intend to proceed with analysis;

Greetings

Great Morning Sexy

Great Night

Hope you are having a good day

How is your day

Just how is such and also such

How are you today

Do not work to tough

What are you doing

I am doing such and such

Thinking about you

I enjoyed last evening

There is nothing in the above messages to engage a woman and build up her tourist attraction. It's just idle conversation. Unless a lady is smitten with a man, these messages will certainly simply make her eyes roll.

While you are sending her those lame messages, there might well be an individual who is shaking her globe with the best words and also techniques. It's the mysterious individual, the one that engages our creativity that presses our buttons.

Suzanne is a carefree, no-nonsense southerly woman. He opened the message with Scarlett, as in O'Hara. What woman would certainly not desire to be seen that way?

That individual recognized exactly how to engage her and also press her switches. She even knew he had paid interest to her. Talk about brushing a lady's ego.

When texting ladies, leave the little talk conversations out of it. If you can't flirt and be lively and make her smile, placed down the phone, or else you are merely tossing cold water on the fire. You intend to problem her to where when she sees it is you texting, she gets thrilled, and her heart avoids a beat. You intend to be the man that she saves his messages.

CHAPTER SIX

Texting Tips to Create Massive Attraction

Neglecting her, and having tons of fish on the line

A lot of men will concentrate only on one woman and at the very same time drive her away, why is this? Now picture you have ten poles in the water, one wiggle; however, you do not give it the same level of interest because two others are showing the rate of interest at the very same time. The more fish you have interested in regarding your lure, the more significant the opportunities you are going to capture one, not only because of a numbers video game yet just since you physically can't also pay much interest to just one.

The Art of Push and Pull

Press and pull I have listened to in the PUA world a few times; however, I have never listened to an excellent explanation as to why it works, and I have never heard it applied to how to text a woman. Allow me to discuss how to relocate this useful tool, so there is no question as to just how to text a girl, flawlessly. (Let me add something, just checked out another "expert's" suggestions on just how to message ladies.

Why you ought to be a pain in the A ** over text.

Being complicated is a killer device for creating attraction over text since it requires the other person to play by your guidelines and not theirs. A whole lot of individuals, when texting a girl, will take an extra natural duty, given that they believe that if she "likes" you, she will undoubtedly choose you. Being challenging and not bowing to the will of a female is compelling and incredibly appealing when texting a woman.

Safety and comfort after that sex.

Above, we chat a lot about pressing her, being demanding, neglecting her, and just elevating your value by not being traditional. At the very same time, it is unbelievably essential to communicate that you are a risk-free individual, that you get along, that you are respectable. That sex is not your top priority. Luckily, massage is a terrific area to do this; with text, you can craft your response rather the knee jerk you might vomit out face to face. Not producing safety and convenience is the primary reason she closes the sex gates on your advancements. If you do not understand precisely how to message a woman appropriately and you send her something that is mildly hostile or excessively sexual, you will undoubtedly set off her flight reaction. Do you recognize why females like gay guys? Because they get their male repair with zero sex-related danger. I am not asking you to be effeminate around women (yet it does not injure) just to comprehend that even the smallest sexual, physical danger sends out ladies running. Exactly how does this convert to texting girls? Straightforward, keep sex speak with a minimum, maintain anger covered up, and existing them the best guy you can. Now mix that with being push/pull, and also you have a guy ALL ladies will be dumb brought in to. (Note, the risk is a kind of sexual stress, but this is a limited rope of tourist attraction, one that can take a lengthy time to master).

Your goal is proficiency, not many strategies and regulations.

I teach a load of rules and methods for texting girls; however, I don't require them anymore. Since I understand the secret of connection balance, something that, if recognized, will introduce you success, not just with texting women but in all relationships.

Should You Text Her? The Rules to Texting Women That You Want to Date.

A great deal of males in today's day and age usually ask yourself whether they ought to message women during the earlier phases of dating. Well, have you merely interesting and attractive female that you want to discover even more regarding? Should you message her?

For starters, when it comes to texting ladies, it would undoubtedly be vital for you to message them back if they message you. Indeed, it would likewise be alright for you to initiate the messages. If you always start the texts, how can you discover out if she is interested in you in return?

You are wrong if you assume that ladies that regularly reply to your text messages are certainly interested in you. Women who let men seek them are typically the ones that will be great with a few days here and there but will not get into connections with any individual. This is simply exactly how females work.

Now, there are likewise a great deal of men around that will certainly text women and maintain texting them till they get a reply. This would not be a good technique. If you make a decision that the solution to "Should you text her?" is indeed, yet she does not respond to you, there is probably a reason behind it - and the reason generally isn't because she didn't receive your texts.

See, even if a woman didn't get your text message, she needs to text you at some time still if she is interested in you, so be a client. Should you message her?

On that note, you should not come and try up with reasons simply to message a female, either. Do not overshare points or be the first to open up with a woman.

So, generally, if you need to know the answer to "Should you text her?", keep in mind that you ought to always so if she texts you. Besides that, just do so if you understand you are doing the right thing to drive her tourist attraction through the roofing system.

For all of you individuals that might have a suitable ability degree with dating women, you may locate on your own regularly getting a telephone number. You head out in the evening with your close friends, wind up meeting a woman at bench or club and have excellent communication, and then you trade contact number. You may be thrilled after this happens, as you may think you have every little thing secured with her. Well, you and lots of others are not even near sealing any kind of take care of her. This is where you require to recognize how to message the woman.

When I first began Getting right into dating, I found that every woman I texted practically never responded to me. This is where you need some excellent text game.

For the ladies that are seemingly intoxicated, you need to message them within minutes, even if you are both still in the club. The ideal attempt would be to duplicate a joke using the message that you both laughed around during your communication. Not all girls get incredibly intoxicated, so below are ideas to have a successful text the next day.

Off, do not listen to anyone that has said to wait a couple of days before texting a girl. You need to message a lady the next day so she can be reminded of the experience you both had. One typical error that guys make and I used to make was just texting monotonous stuff like "Hey," "What's up," and also generic lines like that.

338

To make straightforward, simply experience the funny interactions you had with each other so she can be reminded of your worth. Texting is direct, yet numerous guys wind up losing girls with boring and predictable messages. Make her laugh, and also extra significantly, make her bear in mind why she spoke to you and also the worth you bring to the table as a male.

Do you ever get a woman's phone number and also discover on your shed with what activity to take following?

Let's claim you only me a woman at the bar or cocktail lounge, and also you both clicked and traded telephone numbers. If you do not text her, you want to date this woman and also are frightened you may destroy your chances with her. You message something like ... "Hi, Nice conference you," or "Hey, what's up?".

A lot of people end up losing females they meet because of sending a weak text. Sending out a positive text that will get feedback is very easy! Comply with these actions, and you will be turning your telephone number into dates quickly.

Step 1: Text her something referring to something that occurred between the both of you. This can be a within joke you both had throughout the interaction, or perhaps a commonality. Let's claim during your conversation with the lady; you both learned that you dislike enjoying the news and seafood. You can message her something like, "Hey Jen, wonderful meeting you last night. Let's capture up and also watch the Channel 7 News at some point over some crawfish (smiley face)".

Since it is simply a fast example, yet you understand. It is funny, and also shows that you bear in mind something about her. That sure as hell is most likely to spike her feelings a lot more than an easy text claiming, "Hi there exactly how are you?".

Send her a message that will undoubtedly remind her why you both clicked and also why she enjoyed it with you. A word like the one above is going to advise her of the fantastic experience she had with you and also will certainly make her more likely to text you back.

Action 2: Don't wait as well long to message her! Lots of people make the mistake of waiting too many days to message a female. Text her something that will have her laughing, and don't also wait long!

Step 3: Don't message her excessive. There is absolutely nothing even worse than a clingy person sending out hopeless texts. This will merely lead to no responses. Do not fret if she does not respond after the very first time. Wait a day or 2, and attempt again. Just DON'T sound clingy and determined.

Hopefully, these easy ideas will assist you out in your dating life and reveal you just how to message a lady. By dealing with the straightforward and also usual errors guys are making via text message, you will certainly observe a whole lot even more success with the women you meet.

When Texting Females Comply With Text Rules to Keep Them Thinking About You!

Texting ladies is a terrific method to keep the lines of interaction open, yet there still is message etiquette to comply with to maintain them thinking about you.

You can text ladies, without being so direct by getting the phone, or two indirect by dispatching an email. Text messaging is a terrific method to allow a person to understand you are assuming about them, without stressing that you are disrupting their routine.

When it comes to establishing strategies with a female, it is much better text rules to offer her a call instead of sending her off a text. If you are somewhat interested in a lady, you need to be putting in even more initiative, not less. This indicates not counting on texting as the primary method of interaction.

Texting females works best once you have now established a connection. It's a wonderful way to be teasing, without beginning as well strong. For circumstances, if you had a wonderful very first day with a female, adhering to up with a text that night allows her to know that you had a good time. It assures her that you are interested in her, without making you look as well excited.

The reality that you're touching base with a female is what's important, instead than worrying excessively about what to claim. Ladies like to understand that an individual they're into is thinking of them. Text etiquette has to do with preserving the link, and not regarding building a relationship by message.

Much like with calling or emailing a female, you still don't desire to be sending off way too many texts. Even though texting is a less straight type of communication, you can again encounter as also interested. Maintain some balance by evaluating exactly how frequent her message actions are to you. If she does not react back right away, do not stress.

Texting enables you to be much less inhibited and say something that you would not feel comfortable saying personally, or on the phone. Select up the phone rather if you desire to have a lengthier or even more meaningful conversation with a woman. You will certainly find as a lot more honest.

Being real for text etiquette, constantly be courteous in your messages. Don't use texting as a way to be upset or impolite with a female that rejects you, since it's easy to do it when she can't see you or hear you.

If you feel that what you said did not come throughout precisely, clarify it with her on the phone. New texting can make it worst.

How to Seduce Women on Online Dating Sites - Three Quick Tips to Success

Many men utilize on-line dating solutions not just because it's practical, but additionally, that ladies who are now on-line are 'much easier' to strategy since they are more open to making new pals. Read on to discover three fast pointers you can make use of to be much more reliable at finding your companion online and attain fantastic outcomes quickly ...

Tip Idea 1: "Appear As A NewbieRookie.

Once in a while, edit your online account so that you look that you are 'new.' This will make you a lot more eye-catching - bear in mind that any kind of reasonably 'aged' profile will give the impression that you have been seeking a long, very long time (which is not eye-catching!). Place on some fresh photos which make you look excellent - females often tend to screen our potential partners based on appearances, bear in mind that.

Suggestion # 2: "Similarity Breeds Familiarity." We are all brought in to individuals who resemble us. For that reason, when you zoom right into the profile of somebody you like, take a look at her leisure activities and passions. After that, modify your profile ahead across as somewhat similar to her. This will provide you a boost and also she will feel (subconsciously) that she likes you.

Suggestion # 3: "Hypnosis/ Fractionation". When you get her to talk with you online, it will certainly be useful to use some hypnosis strategies and tricks to make her like you a lot more (and get her intend to go out with you).

This method, called fractionation, has been used by professionals on the internet seducers to make ladies fall in love with them promptly. All you need to do is to make her go through an emotional rollercoaster with your conversation messages - and also 'anchoring' her pleased states with you.

But before you use this strategy, you have to heed this warning.

Fractionation is taken into consideration as a 'dark art' technique, which is the basis of hypnosis-based seduction. Also, while questionable, it is understood to be among one of the most efficient tactics ever before developed by underground reductionists.

It is described in a step-by-step system in the Deadly Seduction Manuscript (http://www.DeadlySeduction.com).

These psychology tactics are very unconventional methods that are used by the secret elite in the seduction Neighborhood. Use it at your own risk. I directly vouch for the efficiency of these tactics, yet care should be taken as they can be outright dangerous in the hands of the unethical.

How to Approach Women? Essential Tips You Need to Know

Due to gender differences, guys usually wait to speak to women. There can be several reasons behind this, but without going into its information, we can say that it has to be gotten rid of, and men need to be educated just how to come close to ladies with confidence. In this short article, we will certainly discuss some vital ideas you need to recognize to find true love. In your daily life, we come across with particular scenarios when we require to connect with women for a variety of reasons. Sometimes we get closer to among them, but quickly because of improper strategy, we have to step back to keep a normal relationship going.

First off, to get the exposure, you need to boost your social circle. This can be done by meeting more people in daily procedures. When you certainly meet extra new individuals in your life, they will certainly last an impact, which aids in building fundamental assumptions towards life. If you have a trendy lady in your course and you intend to date her. The very best method is to ask her to aid you in homework for which you can straight ask for her contact number. Once your relationship expands, it will be simpler interacting over personal issues and chatting regarding likes and disapproval leading towards making long-term love association.

You can go online and start communicating with women over dating sites. It is very vital to create an online account to allow others to see what kind of person you are.

You can ask a specialist who understands about love connections and can direct you over this on exactly how to target ideal resource to locate a real love. Love is something that speeds up an individual's capacity to execute his work. When you are in love, every little thing looks stunning, and also you begin considering points favorably.

CONCLUSION

There's a large amount of nuance in texting. But eventually, it's all about simplicity. The more comfortable your text messages are actually, the better a response they receive. Indeed, there's a great benefit to keeping things simple but very effective. That's why you acquired this book!

I hope that you have learned a lot from the topics covered in this book, and you are indeed ready to try out all the suggestions and tips. Whether it is your very first text to a new girl who contacts you just got or a follow-up text with a girl you haven't talked with in a long while, this book is specially dedicated to your success. Try it with a variety of girls at the very least 5 to 10 phone numbers. The night-and-day distinction in responses you receive will amaze you in positive ways.

Very often in life, certain things occur for a reason, and it's feasible that the women that deny you are doing you a massive favor, likely saving you a whole lot of time, power, and money being spent on the wrong woman for you.

Dating is a result of series activities, so the more phone numbers you get, the additional strategy that you get at conversing and moving closer to women. Your confidence is attached to your continued success with dating the women you develop an interest in.

When working with rejection coming from women when trying to date them, you should definitely not let a stranger possess so much power over you.

CPSIA information can be obtained
at www.ICGtesting.com
Printed in the USA
LVHW100802021120
670426LV00010B/266

9 781801 123020